M000316626

Controller and CFO's Guide to Accounts Payable

Controller and CFO's Guide to Accounts Payable

Mary S. Schaeffer

John Wiley & Sons, Inc.

Published by John Wiley & Sons, Inc., Hoboken, New Jersey.

Published simultaneously in Canada.

For general information on our other products and services, or technical support, please contact our Customer Care Department within the United States at 800-762-2974, outside the United States at 317-572-3993 or fax 317-572-4002.

Wiley also publishes its books in a variety of electronic formats. Some content that appears in print may not be available in electronic books.

For more information about Wiley products, visit our Web site at http://www.wiley.com.

Library of Congress Cataloging-in-Publication Data:

Schaeffer, Mary S.
  Controller and CFO's guide to accounts payable / Mary S. Schaeffer.
    p. cm.
  Includes index.
  ISBN-13: 978-0-471-78589-7 (cloth)
  ISBN-10: 0-471-78589-X (cloth)
  1. Accounts payable. I. Title.

HF5681.A27S32 2007

658.15'26—dc22

                                                           2006016506

Printed in the United States of America

10 9 8 7 6 5 4 3 2 1

For the three people I hope to meet in heaven (should by some miracle, I make it through the pearly gates):

Richard Guillen, my nephew, who was taken from us far too soon
Ron Schacht, my dad, who I continue to miss, and
Thelma Schaeffer, my husband's mother, who I never had the pleasure of getting to know

Contents

Contents

Contents

Contents

Contents

Contents

Contents

Contents

Preface

Many people seeing the title of this book will wonder at its size. After all, they'll think, "What's the big deal? You get a bill and you pay it. How can that possibly take up a whole book?" The answer is quite simple: There's a lot more to accounts payable than just paying bills; this is unless you don't mind:

- Paying invoices twice
- Losing early payment discounts
- Getting in trouble with state auditors
- Being fined by those state auditors
- Tarnishing your vendor relationships
- Spending a lot more on the accounts payable process than is needed
- Getting hit repeatedly with check fraud losses
- Overpaying your vendors
- Running an inefficient and costly operation

There's more, but I think you probably get the picture. While the primary goal of this book is to share information with controllers and CFOs about the myriad of tasks handled in accounts payable, there is a secondary goal as well. Few people, unless they are intimately involved with accounts payable, realize what is involved in "getting an invoice and paying it." In addition to explaining all the tasks that are required to get that process completed in the most cost-efficient manner, I hope to show all the problems that can and do occur during this process.

Often these problems arise not through any bad intentions on the part of those outside the department, but because they simply don't understand. To give you a simple example, let's talk about coding invoices for payment. To be done in a manner that will cause as few problems as possible, everyone must code vendor names exactly the same. Now, you are probably thinking, "control freak central," but let me explain what can go wrong if this standard is not used. Invoices can be paid two or three times, as the system does not recognize the invoice when it gets submitted a second time. Now, if you think that invoices do not get submitted two or three times, let me assure you they do. So, what from the outside may seem like an unreasonable request actually has a strong foundation.

As I go through each of the chapters, I'll explain not only the function, but also what can go wrong and some solutions to help avoid those problems. Also included are lots of best practice advice and insights as to where to look for problems. The book is broken into three segments, the first focusing on the core functionality of any accounts payable operation, followed by a section on specialty functions, and closing with a section on management and oversight issues. The book starts off by addressing the core functions for any accounts payable department. These functions are always handled in accounts payable, the infamous invoice processing and ensuing payment.

Part II of the book turns its attention to specialty functions. Numerous functions (e.g., T&E, Sales and Use Tax, Unclaimed Property, 1099 Reporting, Purchasing cards, and VAT Reclaim) are sometimes handled in accounts payable and sometimes in other departments. There does not seem to be any rhyme or reason for why they are handled sometimes in accounts payable and sometimes not. In this section, we'll delve into each of these issues, again addressing the issues that can sometimes go wrong.

Finally, toward the end of the book, attention is turned toward management and oversight issues. Alas, fraud continues to be a concern, and crooks are forever cooking up new ways to get around the controls that companies develop to thwart them. We'll look at some of the newest initiatives, both on the crooks' side and what companies and banks are doing to stop the problems.

Some of the new technological initiatives being developed are focused on the accounts payable function. These are changing the way the accounts payable function is handled, relieving companies of some of the data-entry tedium that one often thinks of in association with accounts payable. This new functionality has made the process smoother, reduced errors, and freed up accounts payable staff for more value-added functions. Some of those more value-added functions include looking at potential cash management initiatives that will make their organizations more profitable. They also include ways to make the accounts payable process run a little smoother.

It would not be possible to write a book of this type in this day and age without addressing the impact the Sarbanes-Oxley Act has made on the function. While this has been primarily in the area of internal controls, the Act has had an impact in other areas as well. Interestingly, the Act has even forced some companies that are not required to comply with it to rethink some of their internal control issues. The impact of the Act on your accounts payable function is discussed in the last chapter.

Best of luck.

Mary Schaeffer
October 2006

PART I

Core Functions

Part I addresses the basic functions handled in virtually every accounts payable department. Basically this covers the entire procure-to-pay cycle. We begin by looking at the important issue of internal controls. Without appropriate controls, the door to duplicate payments and fraud is opened wide. The section then investigates the invoice handling process as well as the ensuing payment process before delving into the processes that affect the function.

Few people outside of accounts payable understand the negative ramifications of exception processing. By investigating what can go wrong when items are handled outside the normal invoice/payment processing routines, you will understand why it is imperative to minimize the number of exception items allowed.

Another issue that few companies like to talk about in public is the level of duplicate and erroneous payments that occurs at their companies. We'll also provide suggestions to help you minimize this problem.

Handling vendors correctly is also an overlooked issue. Not only vendor relationships, but also the way data related to vendors is handled. The very serious issue of the master vendor file is investigated, and proper techniques are shared.

Finally, there is the question of discounts, early-payment discounts, and the occasional deduction that will be taken against an invoice. Best practices for these issues are discussed because the proper handling of discounts and deductions will affect the productivity of your accounts payable department.

1

Internal Controls in
Accounts Payable

The What-Happens-in-Vegas-Stays-in-Vegas philosophy does not apply to accounts payable or purchasing or treasury or receiving, no matter how much some of these groups would like to operate in their own little fiefdoms. In fact, in this post–Sarbanes-Oxley era, everything is transparent when it comes to corporate operations. This strategy appears to be infiltrating private companies and not-for-profits as well as public companies.

If internal controls and processes break down between accounts payable and purchasing, the ramifications are likely to be felt all the way down to the bottom line. Nothing good can come out of these collapses. Unless they are intimately involved in the nitty-gritty of the accounts payable operations, only a few savvy controllers and CFOs realize the far-reaching impact of just a few poor, seemingly minor, decisions related to the accounts payable process.

Without this insight, many consider the demands of the accounts payable staff to be controlling, not seeing the forest for the trees, or worse. However, I think that when the implications are spelled out, you will realize that the accounts payable manager who demands, for instance, that all invoices be sent directly to accounts payable, is not a control freak but rather one who is concerned about earning early-payment discounts. Similarly, the one who refuses to issue Rush checks in all but the most dire circumstances is not being difficult but rather trying to ensure that the company does not make duplicate payments or, worse, pay a fraudulent invoice.

Now that accounts payable is no longer considered a back-office, non-value-added function, savvy business managers know that in order to run a leading-edge company, it is crucial that proper attention be paid to the accounts payable function. Now, before you turn the page thinking I am making a big fuss over nothing, let me explain what can go wrong when the accounts payable function is ignored. Then we can talk a little bit about the guidelines that will make your company's payment process best-in-class. Before we start, we'd like to point out that in most organizations, accounts payable includes travel and entertainment (T&E), 1099s, unclaimed property, sales and use tax, and value-added tax (VAT) reclaim.

IGNORE ACCOUNTS PAYABLE AT YOUR OWN PERIL

Recently, Wal-Mart and American University were in the news in ways both would probably have preferred to avoid. In the Wal-Mart case, one of its top lieutenants, Tom Coughlin, was accused of expense account abuse. A similar allegation led to the ousting of American University president Benjamin Ladner. In the latter case, the University was so incensed by Ladner's activity that it took unusual action. Newspaper accounts indicate that the University reported Mr. Ladner's excess spending as income to the IRS retroactively. While the amounts of money involved might be high to the average person, the institutions in question can probably afford the hit. What they did not need was the excessive adverse publicity that surrounded these events.

Bad publicity is only the beginning of the negative consequences for poor or weak accounts payable practices. The financial implications can be far more damaging. For starters, poor controls in the accounts payable process can lead to duplicate payments (and, no, the other side does not automatically give the funds back), open the door for fraud, lead to aggravation with state auditing groups, and for public companies, cause trouble with Sarbanes-Oxley audits.

Although most companies don't like to admit it in public, duplicate and erroneous payments are a huge problem in the corporate world. A whole industry has sprung up around the issue. These numerous third-party firms will uncover and retrieve duplicate payments on a contingency basis. While that business has gotten quite competitive in recent years, the fact that this industry exists is a signal of the extent of the problem. A high percentage of these duplicate payments arise from poor practices in accounts payable, purchasing, and receiving, as well as the document flow among the three. In many instances, the accounts payable manager knows the right way to process invoices and payments but lacks the clout to enforce the changes needed to right these wrongs.

THE FRAUD PROBLEM

Fraud can take several shapes. Check fraud is a colossal problem in the United States. Experts estimate that financial institutions lose about $12 billion a year in check fraud alone. And that's just the loss at banks. Now, if you are thinking that you do not have to worry about your check processes because your bank will eat any losses, think again. The problem has gotten so out of control that changes have been made to the Uniform Commercial Code (UCC) to address the problem. Now the loss is borne by the party that was best able to prevent the crime. If a company does not exercise "reasonable care," it will be deemed liable for the loss.

Check fraud is just the beginning of the fraud issue for organizations. Phony invoice fraud has been growing, vendor fraud has always been an issue, and employees who are knowledgeable about weaknesses in existing controls have long been known to exploit those loopholes for personal gain. If you are thinking that most of your employees are long-term trusted individuals, so this is not a problem in your organization, let me share with you a little-known fact. Most employee fraud is committed by long-term trusted employees.

STATE AUDITING GROUPS

Most states are desperate for income and are vigorously looking for ways to increase that income without increasing taxes on the voters who elected the state officials. What may come as a shock is the way the states are generating the shortfalls in their budgets. Two of the techniques could hit your bottom line if your organization is not handling them correctly.

The first is unclaimed property. Every organization is supposed to turn over to the state any unclaimed property it may have. That includes uncashed checks (including payroll). That's right; uncashed checks are supposed to be turned over to the state. Writing these checks off to miscellaneous income is a huge no-no. The relevant dates and amounts vary by state. The much ballyhooed business exemption is so weak, it is rarely worth considering. States are hiring third-party auditors who often work on a contingency basis. These firms often work for more than one state. So if your company is not complying with the rules, it could be audited numerous times as the auditors for each state show up on your doorstep. If the auditors find a shortfall, your organization will not only have to pay what is owed, but it will also be hit with penalties and/or fines. And they audit more than the current year.

A similar situation exists for sales and use tax, where the abuse may not be as high, but the rules are certainly more complex, given the over 7,000 taxing authorities in the United States alone.

SARBANES-OXLEY IMPACT

As public companies across the country struggle with Sarbanes-Oxley (S-Ox) audits, they are discovering that inadequate controls of the accounts payable function will get them dinged in their S-Ox audit. That's right; doing things poorly in your payment process can lead to trouble with Section 404 on Internal Controls. Interestingly, in a recent poll conducted by *Accounts Payable Now & Tomorrow*, a newsletter for professionals interested in payment issues, many companies (both public and private) admitted that they had changed some of their processes as a direct result of the passage of the Act. Over half conceded that they had tightened up their T&E processes.

Not only public companies are affected by the Act. Private companies are being required to conform to the strictures of the Act by key suppliers, key customers, and their financial institutions.

This discussion is not meant to scare those who have been ignoring their accounts payable processes, but rather to serve as a wake-up call before your bottom line is adversely impacted or one of the state auditors shows up on your doorstep with a big, fat penalty bill. Even if your organization can easily afford to pay the fines, who needs that aggravation? Rarely is this seen as a good career move by one's bosses.

A MARRIAGE MADE IN HEAVEN—NOT!

As alluded to previously, purchasing and accounts payable often do not see eye to eye on many issues. Disagreements between accounts payable and purchasing account for a large percentage of the problems that occur in accounts payable. Purchasing wins 90% of these disagreements—often to the bottom-line detriment of the organization. Some of the things purchasing does that cause payment problems include:

- Purchase orders (POs) are not completely filled out
- POs are not given to accounts payable
- POs are issued after invoices are received
- Special deals are negotiated and never communicated to accounts payable
- Invoices forwarded to purchasing for approvals are not reviewed for weeks
- Purchasing tells vendors it had sent approved invoices back to AP weeks earlier when in fact they are still sitting in purchasing

As you might imagine, from accounts payable's point of view, it is unfortunate that purchasing is not encouraged to see the problems that arise in accounts payable when some of these issues are not dealt with. Unfortunately, the ramifications of ignoring these issues transcend hurt feelings in accounts payable. The consequences fall right to the bottom line.

So exactly how should the accounts payable function work, especially in conjunction with purchasing? Let's take a look.

IDEAL ACCOUNTS PAYABLE FUNCTION

The first step in the invoice process starts when an item is ordered and purchasing submits a purchase order. In our ideal world, the PO is sent to the supplier. At the same time, it is either sent to accounts payable or entered into a database that can be accessed by accounts payable. The key factor in making this process work from the start is completely filling out the PO. Just in case I haven't beaten that point into the ground, let me reiterate that many problems in the payment process originate because the PO is not completed but rather submitted with partial information.

The next step in the process revolves around the receiving dock. When the goods arrive, they should be checked against the packing slip to make sure everything that is indicated on the packing slip was in fact delivered. Performance in this arena at many companies is spotty. Some do a magnificent job, but others simply sign off on goods received, never doing any checking whatsoever. The packing slip is then either sent to accounts payable for matching or imaged, and the image is forwarded for use in the payment process.

When the invoice arrives, it is matched to the packing slip and purchase order, and if all is in order, the invoice is paid. The phrase "when the invoice arrives" needs further examination. It is not nearly as simple as it seems.

"WHEN THE INVOICE ARRIVES"

The first salient point that should be addressed is where the invoice should be directed. There is no definitive answer other than that invoices should all be directed to the same place. That destination can either be the accounts payable department or the original purchaser. There are two schools of thought on this issue.

The first recommends that all invoices be directed to the accounts payable department. The department would then forward the invoice to the approver for review. Before being forwarded, the invoice could be logged. In this manner, accounts payable would have a good handle on where invoices were and could field calls from vendors efficiently. This process works very well when electronic invoicing is used. In a paper-based environment, it is a bit more cumbersome.

For the system of sending everything to accounts payable to work, the invoice must be clearly marked with either a purchase order number or the name of the purchaser. Without such delineating information, much time is wasted trying to figure out who ordered the goods in the first place.

In fact, it is a recommended best practice that if an invoice is received without such information it should be returned to the vendor with a polite letter asking for either a purchase order number or the name of the purchaser. By the way, a side benefit of this approach is that it helps weed out fraudulent invoices.

The second school of thought has all the invoices going to the original purchaser. While at first glance it may seem like this makes it easier for accounts payable, as they only have to deal with it once it shows up in accounts payable with the necessary approval, that is not necessarily the case. For starters, when looking for past-due payments, many vendors begin by contacting accounts payable. If accounts payable has no knowledge of the invoice, the staff cannot help the vendor.

In this scenario, accounts payable also has no knowledge of how long an invoice has been sitting in purchasing awaiting the approval from the purchasing manager. Thus, invoices could be seriously delinquent, and the first accounts payable knows of it is when someone demands a Rush check. The issue of Rush checks will be addressed extensively in Chapter 4, Exception Processing.

Another ugly scenario plays out more than occasionally. Here's what happens: Start by recognizing the fact that reviewing an invoice for payment and approving it are pretty low tasks on most purchasing executives' priority lists. So invoices sometimes sit for a long time without being reviewed. Then when the purchasing manager gets the call from the vendor looking for payment, he goes into action.

Not wanting to admit that he is the hold-up, he approves the invoice for payment (without much review) and puts it in the interoffice mail. And what does this genius tell the vendor? Not wanting to look bad. He says something like, "I sent it back to accounts payable weeks ago. I don't know why those guys haven't paid you." Usually, this dialogue is peppered with a few expletives that are not designed to present accounts payable in a favorable light.

In this hypothetical scenario, the vendor now calls accounts payable in a rage because he believes that accounts payable is responsible for his delayed payment. The conversation with the vendor regarding payment in these situations tends to be less than pretty. So, while on the face of it, having invoices go directly to the purchaser may not save accounts payable as much work as it would seem at first glance. In fact, some would argue that, depending on the cooperation from purchasing, it may even increase accounts payable's workload.

Electronic invoicing will be discussed in the following chapter, so we will not go into it in too much detail here. Suffice it to say that the electronic audit trail that is inherent whenever e-mail is used clears up some of these problems.

SEGREGATION OF DUTIES

One of the most critical features when it comes to controls is the appropriate segregation of duties. With the myriad of different responsibilities that fall under the accounts payable umbrella, appropriate segregation of duties, especially in companies with smaller accounts payable departments, can sometimes be a challenge. This is magnified by the fact that it is not always readily apparent what duties should be segregated.

Segregation of Duties & Sarbanes-Oxley

Sarbanes-Oxley raised the bar when it came to the segregation-of-duties issue. While everyone knew it was important, it was one of those issues that sometimes got ignored in some organizations. Inappropriate segregation of duties is one of the issues that allows insider fraud, sometimes referred to as occupational fraud, to occur. The problem here is that companies are sometimes lulled into a false sense of security because the individual

11

who has the duties that are not properly segregated is a trusted employee.

Well, do you know who most frequently commits fraud? Long term trusted employees. So, do not be lulled by the thought that Joe in Accounting has been with you forever and would never do anything to hurt the organization.

Numerous executives have reported that they have been dinged in their Sarbanes-Oxley audit for not having appropriate segregation of duties. By, the way, the other big area that has emerged as an issue for some organizations, is inadequate documentation. It appears that more than a few firms have not updated their policy and procedures manual in quite some time.

If the segregation-of-duties issue becomes a problem within accounts payable because of staffing size, sometimes parties in other departments can be drafted to address some of the issues. For example, someone in treasury or accounting might get checks signed, handle the bank reconciliations, or be responsible for updates to the master vendor file.

CONTROL ON PAYMENT TYPES

As the business world evolves, new payment technologies are emerging to complement the check and wire transfer methodologies that have long been standard. Companies now use purchasing cards and automated clearinghouse (ACH) payments to complement the traditional payment approaches. Overall, these new payment types make the payment process more efficient.

However, if care is not taken, that efficiency can come back and hit an organization in the face. It has long been known that when payments are made by wire transfer by a department other than the one that issues checks, attention must be given to ensure that a check is not also cut. A best practice recommendation in this area is that one payment type be selected for each vendor.

In other words, a vendor can be paid by either check or wire transfer, but not one method for one invoice and then a different one for the next. With the growth of purchase cards (p-cards) and ACH payments in the corporate arena, this problem has mushroomed. Some vendors who accept p-cards are not able to suppress the printing of invoices. Thus, even though the item has been paid for with the p-card, the invoice still gets mailed.

And you know what occasionally happens when the invoice shows up at the company. The purchaser sometimes forgets that he or she paid for the item with a p-card and approves the invoice and sends it off to accounts payable for processing. Sometimes these invoices show in small print that the invoice has been paid for with the p-card and sometimes they don't. Unfortunately, sometimes these invoices are paid a second time by check.

The multiple payment possibilities provide a ripe area for the firms that specialize in finding duplicate payments. It is recommended that each vendor be set up in the master vendor file with only one payment type allocated. Thus, if a vendor is a p-card vendor, checks are never issued to that entity without numerous overrides and approvals from senior management, as well as a very good explanation from the person requesting the policy violation.

OTHER PAYMENT TYPE CONTROL ISSUES

Limiting payment types to one per vendor is one way to eliminate problems. Another is to make sure that information about all payment types is entered into all applicable systems. If really good controls exist around this issue, the question of whether one or more payment mechanisms are used is of less importance. However, in many systems, there is a loophole in this regard.

When the three-way match discussed earlier in this chapter is completed, many systems close the purchase order. However, if a wire transfer is used, this step is often missed, leaving the purchase order outstanding and available for matching if an approved invoice shows up.

OFTEN-OVERLOOKED ISSUE: SPREADSHEETS

Four out of every five organizations use one or more of the Microsoft Office tools (Word, Excel, Access, and Outlook) in their day-to-day operations of the accounts payable operations in a structured manner. These figures come from a recent *Accounts Payable Now & Tomorrow* poll of its readers. As might be expected, the heaviest reliance is on Excel spreadsheets, but other tools are used heavily as well.

What we did find troubling was how these applications are audited, or should we say, not audited. While 53% include these applications in their standard audits, 47% of the respondents do not have these applications audited. This means there are huge "opportunities" for fraud. Let me give you a simple example of what PinPoint Recovery found when auditing one client for duplicate payments.

Some firms track their escheatable items on an Excel spreadsheet. When bank accounts are closed, as they inevitably are, outstanding checks have to be dealt with. Some organizations leave the accounts open until all the checks clear. Typically, a few checks are never cashed. After proper research they may be deemed escheatable. In this case, at the organization in question, the appropriate information was entered onto an Excel spreadsheet, the accounting entries made, and at the appropriate time, the items were turned over to the state. So, what's the problem you ask?

At the firm in question, someone was changing the entries on the Excel spreadsheets. The change did not cost the company a red cent, so its financial records were never affected. What some crafty individual was doing was changing the name of the company to whom the funds were owed to the name of an individual. If this "adjustment" had not been detected, the individual would then have been able to collect the funds free and clear from the state, and no one would have been the wiser.

Since the process of using Office applications in many organizations grew in an informal manner rather than a structured, planned way, the control issue is often overlooked. Many of the applications developed are workarounds that complement the existing accounting package and are used to track issues that are not addressed by the accounting software. Hence, these applications do not always have the strict controls that other functions have.

In fact, when asked about this issue, many of the poll respondents did not have a formal structure in place. More than a few indicated that there were no controls. "We do not have any formal controls in place since these applications (with the exception of Outlook) are used as needed to compile and convey information not readily available from our main AP software," was a typical response.

SPREADSHEET CONTROL PLAN

Normally, disbursement data is entered in and resides on an online accounts payable application where formal and applicable disbursement controls are in place. However, when the accounts payable data source from a desktop application does not contain essential business controls and documented procedures, then there is a real exposure to both fraud and inaccurate payments. Bob Lovallo, president of PinPoint Recovery, advises companies not to overlook this important area. Here are some of the issues that Lovallo says every company needs to consider:

- Are your critical disbursement sensitive data and files residing on a desktop computer that is secure to prevent the introduction of improper data or revision of proper data?
- Are the data and files protected to prevent unauthorized access that can lead to and result in a fraud?
- Are an audit trail and controls in place that support the integrity of source data and file additions, changes, deletions, and output?
- Do you have an inventory list of such disbursement sensitive files and applications?
- If you do have an inventory, have you performed an ongoing security check and audit for data integrity by determining the correctness of the source data?
- Do you have desk procedures that also include a flowchart indicating what control points are in place to ensure that control and auditability is evident and maintained?
- Do your procedures also address and maintain appropriate segregation of duties?
- Have you tested a portion of original source documents, formulas, report computations, and controls to the desktop application's output?

It is important that information at every step of the process have the appropriate controls in place. You will need to verify the input, the calculations, and the output.

POLICY AND PROCEDURES MANUAL

Because many accounts payable departments have grown gradually or evolved as part of the accounting department, few have a written game plan. Instead, procedures are developed on an as-needed basis, in kind of a hodgepodge manner. Moreover, much of the knowledge about how things work and where information is located often resides with specific individuals. If those individuals get sick or accept another job, the company is left in a lurch.

Every accounts payable department should have a procedures manual, to serve not only as a guide in case of emergency, but also to provide managers with the necessary documentation to demonstrate to management the capabilities of the staff and the work they are handling. Without such a document, few understand the scope of information that is needed to run a successful department. This is especially important for those organizations subject to the strictures of S-Ox.

The procedures manual can also be used to determine whether any processes can be eliminated. Needless to say, this document will not be the most interesting book ever written, but it is essential. As an added benefit, it will make the auditors happy.

The manual should not only be prepared by those who are actually doing the day-to-day tasks, but it should also be updated regularly. Some choose to do this anytime a process is amended or added, whereas others do it annually. It is imperative that this be done. You'd be surprised to discover just how much processes change over the course of a year.

There is one other reason to have this manual and insist that everyone follow it. Left to their own devices, processors in accounts payable will gradually develop their own procedures. Without a careful and periodic review, each person will end up handling transactions differently. There is a word for this, and it is *chaos*. If one processor has an idea for an improved way of doing a particular task, the suggestion should be raised with the manager. If it is determined that the suggestion is superior to the methodology in use, everyone should change how they handle that particular task, and the policy and procedures manual should be updated to reflect this change.

Now, if this seems to be a cumbersome and costly task, think again. Thanks to the Internet, many companies now post their manuals on their corporate intranet site. This makes it available to anyone who may need to check it. It also makes updating a snap, and there are no costly printing charges each time the manual is updated. Finally, putting all the latest changes on the intranet removes that old chestnut of an excuse: "nobody told me." E-mail alerts can be sent to everyone who is affected each time the policy is updated.

If your accounts payable department does not have a policy and procedures manual, the staff should bite the bullet and prepare one. If topics are divided among the staff and each one writes a chapter or two, the work will not seem overly burdensome.

If you need some samples, do a search on the Internet. You'll come up with numerous samples that you can modify to fit your own procedures. One word of caution regarding those Internet policies, however: Most are written by universities. If you are in a manufacturing environment, you may have to add several sections. Still, having something to start with is a big help.

Finally, once the manual is completed, especially if it includes your T&E procedures, all affected parties should be notified that they will be expected to conform to the policies. Expect a certain amount of complaining. To make sure the policy is enforced, the first notice to the staff should come from a high-level executive (e.g., the controller or the CFO). Some companies put a short note from this executive on the front page of the policy so everyone understands that they will be expected to adhere to it. This is especially important when it comes to issues like T&E, Rush checks, and not returning checks to requisitioners.

BAD CONTROL PRACTICES

- Not closing purchase orders when payments are made via wire transfers

- Allowing purchase orders to be partially filled out
- Not employing appropriate segregation of duties
- Lack of appropriate oversight and controls over spreadsheet applications
- Allowing a poor working relationship between accounts payable and purchasing to fester

RECOMMENDED MANAGEMENT ACTIONS

- Take Section 404 of S-Ox seriously, even if you are not required to.
- Insist on proper flow of information to accounts payable from all parties.
- Establish a protocol regarding where invoices are sent.
- Update your accounts payable policy and procedures manual regularly.

2

Invoice Handling

Without a doubt, invoices are the crux of any accounts payable operation. While the many other varied topics that can fall under the accounts payable umbrella are sometimes assigned to other departments, invoice handling is always an accounts payable function. This seemingly innocuous document can give rise to numerous difficulties, even when handled correctly. And when handled in an inappropriate manner, the number of problems skyrockets.

THREE-WAY MATCH

The three-way match revolves around three key documents: the invoice, the purchase order (PO), and the receiving document.

1. *Invoice*—simply put, the invoice is a bill. Invoices can be simple or complex. For example, a bill for a magazine subscription usually has one item on it and is straightforward. However, many invoices are not that simple. They cover numerous items, which are typically listed on the

invoice. These generally are referred to as line items. In addition to information about what was purchased, the invoice will ideally at a minimum:

- Tell where to send the payment
- Indicate when the payment is due
- Delineate payment terms (i.e., show whether a discount is available if a payment is made early)
- Include any special instructions

2. *Purchase order*—this is the document the purchasing department sends to the supplier when ordering goods for the company. Ideally, it will show not only all the details relating to the purchase (i.e., quantity, price) but also any special terms that the buyer may have negotiated. All too often, the purchasing department negotiates a great deal and then forgets to notify the accounts payable department. Then when the vendor "forgets" to use the negotiated price and sends a bill with the original price, accounts payable has no way of knowing and ends up paying the original price—so much for the great negotiation.

   In an ideal world, the purchasing department sends along a copy of all completed purchase orders to accounts payable. In reality, accounts payable does not always receive copies of purchase orders. Also, in many organizations the purchase order is not completely filled out, so even if accounts payable receives the purchase order, it does not have all the information it needs to verify purchases.

3. *Receiving documents*—Before paying an invoice, most companies want to make sure the goods were received. Additionally, they want to know whether everything that was ordered was actually sent. In some industries, suppliers are permitted to ship within tolerances, say 5%. In other words, the supplier can ship anywhere from 5% below the amount ordered to 5% above it. Thus, before paying

the invoice, the accounts payable associate needs to know the quantity received.

The fact that the receiving documents are used in verifying information before a payment is made should put additional pressure on the staff that works on the receiving dock. However, in reality, some receiving departments don't check the goods received against the receiving documents.

The three-way match involves matching these three documents to ensure that everything that was ordered was received, everything that is billed for has been received, and the pricing and terms are correct.

In a perfect environment, where all documents were checked and completed and sent to accounts payable, paying invoices would be rather simple. The accounts payable associate takes the three governing documents—the invoice, the purchase order, and the receiving document—and compares them. If they all agree, then the invoice could be processed for payment. The first-time match rate at many companies hovers in the 50% area. The first-time match rate is also sometimes referred to as a first-time hit rate.

That's right; only half the invoices that come in for payment match the purchase order and the receiving documents. This is not to say that many companies do not have first-time hit rates much higher. Many do. If you ask accounts payable professionals in the trenches, they will tell you that the biggest problem is with the invoices.

COMMON INVOICE PROBLEMS AND SOLUTIONS

The simplest solution to many of the problems that will be discussed is to send the invoice back to the vendor and ask them to produce it accurately and using good invoice practices. This is not a viable solution in many cases because most companies generally do not allow this procedure. Here's a look at a number of common invoice problems, along with one or more ways to address the issue so it doesn't bog down the accounts payable process.

Invoices without Invoice Numbers

Of all the problems to be discussed, this is the biggest. While it may seem trivial to those not involved in accounts payable, it is a huge issue. Most organizations use the invoice number as a key determinant for tracking whether a payment for a specific item has been made. Most duplicate payment checking routines focus on the invoice number. Yet, some experts estimate that over 40% of all invoices do not have an invoice number. So, you can see that invoices lacking an invoice number do present a real problem.

It is recommended that invoices without invoice numbers be assigned an invoice number that is created by the accounts payable department. The number should be unique for each invoice. Hence using the date is generally not a good idea unless it is combined with some other unique identifier.

The routine for assigning invoice numbers to invoices without them should be uniform within the department. No one method for assigning numbers is better than all others. The important features are that a routine be developed that generates unique assigned invoice numbers and that everyone in the department uses the same routine.

Critical Point: One really bad way to create a unique identifier is to use the vendor's taxpayer identification number (TIN) along with some numbering scheme. While this approach may generate a unique identifier, it could introduce other problems. The TIN for all employees and some smaller suppliers is their social security number. Given privacy concerns and identify theft difficulties, it is best to avoid any process that could exacerbate these problems.

Small-Dollar Invoices

Small-dollar invoices present accounts payable with unique challenges. They clog up the available processing resources while adding little value. Yet, they must be processed. To eliminate as many of these invoices as possible while still maintaining processing standards, companies can take one or more of the following approaches:

- Insist that purchase cards (p-cards) be used to pay for as many low-dollar items as possible.
- Use negative assurance for these items (see previous description).
- Have employees pay for these items themselves and reimburse them through the T&E process.
- If there are numerous such items (say, from an overnight delivery company), begin paying from the monthly statement and not the individual invoices. Once this step is taken, only pay from the statement and never the invoice.

Invoices without Purchase Order Number or Purchaser Identified

This can be a nightmare for accounts payable. An invoice shows up with no indication as to who ordered the product. This puts the associate processing the payment in a bad way because he or she does not know if the goods were ordered legitimately, and if they were, who should approve the invoice. Some such invoices are completely fraudulent. The best policy, which some companies refuse to adopt, is to send the invoice back. We call it the No PO, No Name: Guess What? No Check policy. In fact, some accounts payable professionals who take this approach report that their vendors understanding this refuse to take orders without a PO number.

A more polite way to address the situation is to develop a form letter to send back to the vendor asking for either a PO number or the name of the purchaser. Depending on your organization's corporate culture and approach to vendors, you may want to keep track of all such requests.

Without the ability to go back to the vendor, accounts payable is left to guess as to who ordered the goods. This can lead to a long, arduous, and inefficient process as the processor tries to track down the purchaser. When the purchaser is finally identified, some insist that a PO be filled out. An after-the-fact PO adds little value and just prolongs an already ineffective process. However, if the purchasers know they will have to fill out a PO regardless, they may be less apt to take the upfront short cut of neglecting to fill out the PO in the first place. This, of course, assumes that the purchase in question should have had a PO.

Invoices That Don't Match the PO

This one's a beaut, and it happens all the time in organizations that tolerate rogue purchasers. An invoice shows up in accounts payable, usually with terms that are different than those on the PO. It may indicate that the customer should pay freight charges when this is normally picked up by the supplier, or some other feature that is not attractive to the customer. When the accounts payable associate calls the customer to get the invoice corrected, they are informed that "Joe in purchasing said it was okay." Sometimes it is simply paying the customer faster than normal without any sort of a financial incentive to do so. This can happen at the vendor's fiscal year-end.

Now one of two things is going on here, and accounts payable usually knows which without having to verify, although they should verify before making any accusations. In the first case, the vendor is trying to pull a fast one and Joe told them no such thing. To address this issue, simply contact Joe and either have him fix the matter or conference in the customer. In fact, if you know the customer is trying to pull the wool over your eyes, conference Joe in on the spot.

The second case is more difficult. In this instance, Joe really did tell the vendor that your company would pay whatever the odd item was. No matter how aggravating this may be to accounts payable, it is not something that most accounts payable managers can resolve. The matter should be escalated to a higher level, say the controller, who will deal with it. Accounts payable's role in this issue is to make management aware of the problem and then follow up on management's instructions in this matter.

Duplicate Invoices

When a vendor does not receive payment within a reasonable amount of time, most likely 30 days, the vendor will initiate collection efforts, including sending a second invoice. This invoice should have the same invoice number as the first invoice, although a few sly vendors will change the invoice number. Sometimes, it is not the vendor trying to pull a fast one, but rather an internal numbering scheme that adds a digit to indicate the invoice is not the original.

The problem for accounts payable is that both invoices may end up being approved and processed for payment. To avoid paying such invoices (which may have been generated in a completely ethical attempt to collect funds owed), incorporate one or more of the following routines into your invoice handling process:

- Perform a duplicate invoice number check before payments are released
- Check dollar amounts and invoice numbers against payments made in the last 90 days

- Verify all payments being made on invoices more than 60 days old
- Make sure your company uses a naming convention when setting up vendors in your Master Vendor Files
- Check all large payments
- Never pay from a copy, without increased verification as discussed in the next section

Invoice Copies

To avoid some of the problems discussed previously, some companies simply refuse to pay from copies. They insist on only paying the original invoice. While this requirement makes sense in a theoretical sense, the mail does occasionally get lost, people spill cups of coffee making documents completely illegible, and all sorts of other mishaps do occur. Thus a policy of never paying from a copy is not realistic. Accounts payable needs to ensure that if they do pay from a copy, the original will not show up a few days later (as they more than occasionally do). How can they do this? Basically, there are a variety of ways, most of which involve making it difficult for someone to request a payment from a copy unless they have a very good reason. Some approaches that might work are:

- Double-check the files to ensure that the invoice has not been paid.
- Require that the request for payment from a copy be signed by a high-level executive. When faced with this task, many people search their desk a little harder and suddenly find the original.
- Pay from a copy only after the invoice is 30 or 60 days old.
- Hold on to the invoice for an additional five to seven days to see if the original "mysteriously" appears. You'll be surprised how often this happens.

Fraudulent Invoices

Unfortunately, many individuals would rather spend their time trying to bilk honest organizations out of their money rather than putting in an honest day's work. These crooks capitalize on the knowledge that accounts payable departments are overworked and do not usually have the resources to devote adequate attention to small-dollar invoices. Sometimes they will deliver shoddy or low-quality goods to a company, and these companies bill them for those products at inflated prices. A few of the more outrageous thieves will even try to aggressively collect on these invoices. The most common schemes involve copier paper, toner for copy machines, help wanted advertisements, and yellow pages ads.

Some of these invoices will fall into the category of no PO number, no requisitioner, and with good reason, because no one ordered the goods. That's why a "No PO, No check" policy works well. It stops these people in their tracks. Insisting on a PO for all goods is another way to eliminate these invoices from phantom vendors.

Now if you are thinking that it is no big deal for most organizations if they pay a $25 invoice that is fraudulent, you are both right and wrong. While the bottom-line impact of that one invoice is small, there are bigger implications. Few fraudulent vendors willingly walk away from a gravy boat. The company that pays one invoice will receive additional ones. Good upfront vendor verification programs will also help nip this problem in the bud.

Disputed Invoices

Invoices with numerous discrepancies are referred to as either disputed invoices or discrepant invoices. Some companies take the stance that they will not pay the invoice until all disputes are completely resolved. This has the advantage in that the customer can then accurately apply cash to the right outstanding invoice. It also ignores the financial reality for the vendor, who may not be able to wait that long for its payments. A few unscrupulous companies refuse to make partial payments as a way of enhancing their own cash flow. However, these are limited.

The key with disputed invoices is to resolve the discrepancies quickly, ideally before the payment is due. If a partial or short payment is made, the reasons for the deductions should be spelled out for the vendor. If the explanation is not included, the vendor may:

- Apply cash incorrectly
- Apply the cash to another customer (Yikes!)
- Call the accounts payable department for an explanation
- Put the customer on credit hold

None of these outcomes are desirable, and all will result in additional work for accounts payable when the vendor calls looking for the shortage. A best practice approach for dealing with disputed invoices should include:

- Resolve disputes before the due date. If an online dispute resolution mechanism is available, use it. If not, take advantage of existing technologies to force a discussion and resolution.
- If short payments are made, communicate the reasons for the deductions with the vendor.
- Document your reasons for short payments, and make sure they are readily accessible long after the fact.

While these practices will help keep the disputed invoice process under control, your long-term goal should be to reduce these disputes. One way to do that is to track disputed invoices to identify trends and weaknesses in the process. Some of the metrics you might want to track to identify process loopholes are:

- Number of disputes by vendor
- Number of disputes by purchaser
- Number of disputes by type
- Number of disputes by location

If you see an inordinate number of disputes in one or two areas, you can then focus on what's going wrong in the process there. Alternatively, if you note that a few purchasers or locations have few or no disputes, you can investigate what that location/person is doing differently than the others. After a thorough analysis, you might want to make their process a best practice in your organization.

Recurring Invoices

Almost every organization has payments that it makes each month for the same item for the same dollar amount. Common examples include rent, lease payments, and loan payments. Efficient accounts payable departments do not go through the complete invoice approval process each month for these payments. They set them up so they are automatically made, either by having the check cut through the check production cycle or by initiating a wire transfer.

Accounts payable must address several issues when setting these payments up so they do not continue making these payments when the obligation no longer exists. This is most obvious with loan and lease obligations but can also happen with rent for a facility that is not part of the main locale.

In addition to putting in place a mechanism that stops the payment when the obligation is fulfilled, accounts payable needs also to be included in a reporting mechanism so that if the obligation is terminated early, they are informed and stop the payments.

Some organizations set up blanket POs to address the first issue, that of the obligation's natural life. Others set up the

31

blanket PO to cover only a calendar year and review all blanket POs annually to determine if they should be reset. This annual review sometimes catches obligations that were terminated early.

Illegible Invoices with Vague Information

Most companies end up with a few invoices, usually from small suppliers, that leave much to be desired. They are handwritten, and sometimes the paper they are written on is whatever the vendor had on hand. If the vendor in question is a craftsperson or contractor, the paper on hand might even be a paper bag. Suggesting to this person that you would like them to use one of the online billing services is not going to get you far. Many will not even have a computer. While this problem is diminishing, it still exists.

Accounts payable professionals can take several steps to fix this problem, depending on how involved they want to get. They can accept the invoice on the paper bag and process it when they get around to it, but that may not be the best approach. You know this brown paper bag invoice does not have an invoice number.

The kind-hearted processors will take a few sheets of paper and design an invoice and give it to the vendor. Resist the impulse to put an invoice number on this piece of paper. Why? In all likelihood, if the vendor is not offended, he or she will copy that piece of paper. If you have included an invoice number, you will end up with numerous invoices with the same invoice number.

Invoices with vague information require a different approach. One accounts payable professional reported that one of her vendors was including guesstimates for freight charges. Clearly, that approach is not appropriate. Where possible, vendors who submit unprofessional invoices should be directed to some of the online billing services. Some of these are inexpensive and can provide a professional touch.

Invoices That Don't Reflect Special Deals

The value of special deals negotiated by a fine purchasing staff can be completely lost if the information is not communicated to accounts payable. If purchasing doesn't notify accounts payable, the company will only accrue the benefits if everything is in order on the supplier's side. Who wants to rely on the supplier to make sure that your organization gets the best price or terms?

First, in order for you to even discern that you have a problem in this area, you'll need to ensure that your purchasing guys are filling out purchase orders completely. Otherwise, you'll never even know that you have a problem. Good relations with purchasing helps in this area. If an invoice shows up with terms or prices that are more advantageous than your standard terms, try and schedule a meeting with the purchasing executive responsible for the order in question. One of three things could have happened:

1. The invoice could just be incorrect.
2. The supplier could be giving better terms to other customers. If this is the case, your purchasing department should have this intelligence so it can negotiate better terms or prices for your organization.
3. Your purchasing group could have negotiated a special deal and "forgot" to notify accounts payable.

Once an invoice shows up that does not reflect a special deal, it becomes a disputed invoice. Disputed invoices typically take longer to get paid than ones that match the PO. One of the old chestnuts in accounts payable is that "a good bill gets a good check." Thus, it is in your supplier's best interest to get the invoice issued correctly. Communicate this fact to them.

Getting the supplier to reflect special deals on your invoices correctly the first time will probably take some help from your purchasing department. A concerted effort by purchasing and accounts payable is your best defense against a supplier who neglects to include these specials on invoices.

Occasionally, when the special deals involve a discount for early payment, the supplier will intentionally leave the information off, making it difficult for your organization to earn that discount. In our opinion, this is negotiating in really bad faith, although proving it will be another matter. Read the following section for tips in this regard.

By the way, if you have certain suppliers who routinely (say, every year-end) offer special deals, you might create a list of these suppliers and then check their invoices closely at those key times. In certain industries, this occurs at year-end. If this is the case in your industry, watch your January invoices—just the time when accounts payable doesn't have tons of extra time. You might send a quick note to the purchasing manager asking for a list of these special deals, if you suspect that they were not included on the POs. This might be your first step toward having accounts payable do contract compliance, but that's a whole different story.

Invoices Mailed Late

This can be ugly. Occasionally, an accounts payable department will find that despite implementing best invoice processing practices, several vendors' invoices are never processed in time to take advantage of the early-payment discounts offered. In organizations where missing the discount is treated like committing a mortal sin, this is a serious issue.

The first step is to evaluate your own processes to see if some internal snag is causing the problem. Do these invoices have to go to an executive in purchasing for approval, who typically takes days to handle any paperwork? Is the invoice addressed to the proper person or department? Do your processors have a backlog that is causing a processing delay? After you have identified every possible flaw in your processes and eliminated them all, turn your attention toward the vendor.

Start by keeping the envelopes that the invoices are mailed in. (If you already do that, dig them out and get started.) Compare the invoice dates to the date stamped on the envelope at the post office. Is there a discrepancy? A few unscrupulous vendors have been known to hold back mailing these invoices, making it impossible for the customer to earn that early-payment discount.

A word of caution: Even if you determine that the invoices have been held, proceed gingerly. Here's why: A few vendors review invoices before mailing them to ensure that they are accurate. You don't want to accuse a vendor who is trying to do the right thing of trying to shortchange you. However, if the vendor is holding the invoices to review them for accuracy, that should not be your problem and should not affect the time you have to process an invoice. If this is being done, you can either negotiate a change in terms or negotiate that the discount period will start from the postmark date.

One other thought: Even if your vendor is purposely holding invoices, it probably is not a good idea to get into an out-and-out argument over it. Better to take the high road and act like you think they are holding the invoices to verify them rather than to make it difficult for you. By approaching this in a nonaccusatory style, you may be able to resolve the situation while allowing the scoundrels to save face, which you probably should do if you are going to continue doing business with this organization.

This discussion will probably have to involve someone from your purchasing staff. In fact, the purchasing professional responsible for the relationship may need to have the conversation. Just make sure they understand all the implications of the delayed mailing.

ALTERNATIVE TO THREE-WAY MATCH: EVALUATED RECEIPT SETTLEMENT

The folks who developed the Evaluated Receipt Settlement (ERS) approach to the procure-to-pay process honed in quickly on the fact that the invoice is typically the biggest cause of problems in the payment and matching cycle. They also reflected on the fact that it was the most useless document if everything else was done correctly—a big if, I'll grant you.

Let's look at the process as it is supposed to work. A company places an order by submitting a PO. The PO not only contains information about the goods ordered (e.g., quantity, size, price, color), but it also should have payment terms. Now, let's look at the receiving end. When the goods come in, there is a packing slip. It should contain complete information about what was delivered, and the receiving staff should verify that the information on the packing slip matches exactly the goods that are delivered.

In theory, at this point, the company has all the information it needs to pay the vendor. It knows when the goods were received and the agreed-upon payment terms. So, what added value does the invoice bring? None, say proponents of ERS, who advocate simply paying the vendor based on this information. This is what a few companies, most notably those in the automotive industry, do.

For ERS to work, the PO and receiving functions have to be impeccable. Both vendor and customer have to agree to use it. Several issues need to be addressed, most notably the lack of an invoice number, which is used by some as a key determinant for tracing.

ALTERNATIVE TO THREE-WAY MATCH: NEGATIVE ASSURANCE/ASSUMED RECEIPT

Small-dollar invoices present unique challenges to accounts payable. They need to be processed, yet it is not an efficient use of time to spend a lot of time verifying the legitimacy of the invoice and the information on them. However, if they are routinely paid with no verification, a company would find itself inundated with small-dollar fraudulent invoices. While some organizations try and force as many of these payments as possible onto p-cards, that solution is not always available. Whether the company doesn't use p-cards or the vendor doesn't accept credit cards, most organizations must deal with this gap.

Rather than devote the same resources to a $25 invoice as they would a $1,000,000 invoice, the concept of negative assurance emerged. The first part of this process is to set a dollar limit for invoices to be paid using this process. Some companies start small and then increase it. We know of one organization that uses it for all invoices less than $5,000.

An e-mail, sometimes along with a copy of the relevant invoice, is sent to the person who ordered the goods or services. The recipient then has 10 business days to respond to accounts payable to indicate that the invoice should not be paid or should be recoded. If there is no response, the system "assumes that the invoice is legitimate" and releases the invoice for payment against its payment terms.

Another innovation is the move to an image availability of the invoice via the intranet/e-mail platform. With this mechanism in place, no copies need to be sent, but if the recipient had any questions about the item, he or she can view an image of it on the company's intranet.

STATEMENTS

Vendor statements can be either a blessing or a curse, depending on how they are used. The problems with statements start when processors pay based on the statement. This is normally not a good idea, except in one circumstance discussed as follows. If a payment is made based on a statement and the invoice subsequently shows up, the invoice is usually scheduled for payment. Whether it gets paid a second time depends on how good the duplicate payment checking routines are at the firm and if the system has a control that prevents an invoice number from being paid more than once.

But statements definitely do have a very useful place in accounts payable if they are used correctly. Best practices recommend that statements be requested from vendors periodically, depending on workload. Probably the best frequency is quarterly, although some companies do it monthly and others do it annually. Still others request statements from one-quarter of their vendors each month or quarter. In that manner, they cover all vendors in either a year or a quarter.

The important issue when requesting vendor statements is to insist that the statement include all activity. The reason for this is quite simple. More than a few vendors will suppress customer credits from printed statements unless instructed otherwise. Your organization should review all statements and take the credits in a manner that will not disrupt other accounts payable activity. This may mean that you request the vendor cut a check, or you may take a credit on a subsequent invoice. Whichever approach you take, make sure and document what is done. Otherwise, you could have a supplier tying up your accounts payable associates' time trying to collect funds that were correctly taken against an invoice.

PAYING FROM STATEMENTS

Statements have a use in accounts payable, but they can sometimes cause problems. Some vendors send statements monthly to remind their customers of their outstanding obligations. It is generally considered a good policy for accounts payable to request statements from all vendors, asking that these statements include all activity. The reason to emphasize all activity is that some vendors will conveniently forget to include outstanding credits, as mentioned previously.

Unfortunately, when these statements get to accounts payable, a few processors, especially new ones who may not have been adequately trained, will mistake the statement for an invoice and pay it. Thus, invoices get paid twice. Others will identify unpaid invoices on the statements and pay them. Then when the original invoice eventually shows up approved for payment, you know what happens. Thus, many organizations have a policy of never paying from statements.

However, there is at least one instance when paying from statements might be a good idea. As discussed earlier, paying vendors who would normally send numerous small-dollar invoices from a statement might not be a bad idea. To make this practice work effectively, vendors who are paid from statements should only be paid that way. It's an all-or-nothing proposition. Otherwise, chaos, in the form of duplicate and triplicate payments, will occur.

A WORD ABOUT CREDITS

Some vendors are very honorable when it comes to credits. They will send a credit memo to their customers, alerting them to the funds they are owed. Unfortunately, some accounts payable processors still do not fully understand what credit memos are. Their lack of understanding is compounded by lack of knowledge on the part of the purchasing professional. When the credit memo shows up, the purchasing professional approves it for payment and the associate in accounts payable processes it.

With this action, the amount owed to your company now doubles. Yes, that's right; a few processors out there will pay credits. Make sure your accounts payable staff is educated about credits.

GETTING APPROVALS

As alluded to in the prior chapter, sometimes accounts payable has problems getting invoices approved for payment in a timely manner. Typically, invoices are forwarded to the purchaser for approval before going through the three-way match. If the invoices are not returned quickly, the organization can lose its early-payment discount. Additional processing problems occur if the approval is severely delayed.

This leads to friction between purchasing and accounts payable and frequently makes accounts payable look like it is not doing its job, when nothing could be further from the truth. If this is a problem in your organization, ask that accounts payable keep a log for several months showing when an invoice was sent out for approval and when it was returned. If the average time difference is more than a few days, the problem lies outside accounts payable.

If invoices are not originally sent to accounts payable but only arrive there after approvals have been given, ask accounts payable to track invoice date versus the date the invoice is received in accounts payable. Allowing for a few days for mail time and a few days for approval, the difference between the invoice date and the date it is stamped into accounts payable should be less than 14. If it is higher, there is a problem somewhere outside accounts payable. You will need further investigation to determine if the problem is in purchasing or on the part of your vendors. Here's a hint: It is unlikely that all of your vendors are holding onto invoices and mailing them late.

STAMPING MAIL IN ACCOUNTS PAYABLE

Many accounts payable departments date-stamp all mail as it is received into accounts payable. This is a good idea because it helps delineate when invoices were received in case of a dispute. It also helps establish a timeline of when invoices arrived where. Now, we will stipulate that just because an invoice is stamped in on a given date, does not mean that it was sent out for approval that same day. But it does help show, once invoices are returned to accounts payable, if there is adequate time for processing.

Sometimes the invoice gets back in plenty of time, but the procedures, discussed in the following chapter, related to getting the check signed and out the door, bog down the process. If your organization takes several days or longer to get checks signed and released, you may need to print checks earlier in the payment cycle if you want to avoid irritating your suppliers.

ELECTRONIC INVOICING

Electronic invoicing, also referred to as e-invoicing and electronic billing, has made a big dent in the way invoices are handled in the corporate world. As you will see, it also helps end some of the petty problems discussed earlier. Technically speaking, the soup-to-nuts concept is referred to as electronic invoice presentment and payment (EIPP). It refers to the concept of an invoice being sent electronically, received electronically, and the ultimate payment being made electronically most frequently through the ACH.

E-invoicing encompasses many different formats and approaches. At its simplest, e-mailing an attached Word, Excel, or PDF document should be considered electronic invoicing, as the document has arrived electronically at the customer. Similarly, a company that pays its employees using direct deposit is making electronic payments. In each of the examples mentioned, the companies involved are participating in EIPP, albeit in a minor way.

As you have probably figured out, e-invoicing has a positive impact in numerous ways. In addition to the elimination of paper, companies like e-invoicing because:

- Mistakes are reduced, as there is no need to rekey information.
- The workflow to route invoices for approval is easier.
- Costs are reduced.
- Blaming accounts payable for others' own shortcomings in processing paper becomes difficult.

Unfortunately, e-invoicing has not been adopted by everyone immediately. Some of the reasons it has not been embraced as much as might be anticipated include:

- Cost
- Implementation time
- Budget constraints
- Internal resistance to change
- Lack of ease of use
- Difficulty in signing up partners
- Fear

By supporting the use of e-invoicing wherever possible, you will have taken a giant step toward eliminating some of the problems in accounts payable as well as the friction points with other groups within the company. The benefits, as described earlier, make it an approach that should be encouraged. Invoices can be:

- Picked up at the supplier's Web site (seller-centric)
- Delivered by the supplier to the purchaser's Web site (buyer-centric)
- Picked up at a consolidator site (consolidator model)

BAD PRACTICES

- Not tracking where invoices are at all times
- Allowing game playing to go on between different departments
- Not demanding that vendors indicate a PO number or the name of a purchaser on an invoice
- Paying from statements when that is not the policy for that vendor
- Paying credits rather than taking them
- Not having one policy regarding where invoices should be directed

RECOMMENDED MANAGEMENT ACTIONS

- Encourage the use of electronic invoicing
- Insist on a consistent invoice policy
- Work to ensure a smooth working relationship between purchasing and accounts payable

3

Payment Processing and Alternatives

Payment mechanisms used by businesses include the paper check, wire transfers, purchase cards (p-cards), and automated clearinghouse (ACH) payments. At this point in time, the most common form of payment in the United States is the paper check. And, boy, do paper checks cause problems—for accounts payable departments, for their companies when crooks play games, and increasingly for their banks. The check production process, including printing the check, handling the check stock, and getting checks signed and out the door, also has to be handled carefully. If not, problems will multiply. This chapter contains a lot of information about checks. To the uninitiated it may seem like overkill, but consider this: It is your company's money, and handled incorrectly it could result in a serious blow to the bottom line.

CHECK STOCK

Companies use one of two types of checks. The first type is pre-printed with all the requisite banking and company information on them. Typically, these are on a continuous form and have a carbon copy or two that companies file with the backup. Extra care must be taken with storage and printing if this type of check is used. While these checks can be printed on a regular desktop printer, they are most frequently used with mainframe computers.

The other type of check stock is used with laser printers just like the one you may have with your personal computer. It has none of the information printed on it, although some organizations do order paper with their logo preprinted on it. The information, both about the company (e.g., name, address) and banking (e.g., magnetic ink character recognition [MICR] line, bank name, check number) are printed at the time the check is printed. Thus, this type of check stock does not require the same care as preprinted check stock. In fact, although this is not recommended, these checks can even be printed on plain white copier paper. Typically, the check stock used in these cases is referred to as safety paper. It incorporates certain check fraud prevention features.

Some companies use numbered safety paper, which is a recommended best practice. This paper is numbered and incorporates many safety features. Each piece of paper is sequentially numbered. A log is kept of the sequentially numbered safety paper. By itself, the paper is worthless. However, with the right software, it can be turned into a valuable commodity—a negotiable check. When it comes time to print checks, the number of checks to be printed should be calculated. The safety paper is removed from the secure location, the first number of the sequentially numbered paper is noted, and the checks are printed. The last number of the sequentially numbered paper is noted. A calculation should be made, based on the beginning number, the number of checks printed, the ending number, and any ruined sheets of paper, to ascertain that no additional checks were printed. It is especially important to collect any allegedly damaged paper and destroy it.

CHECK STORAGE

Blank checks may look innocuous enough, but in the wrong hands they can cause a lot of damage. A thief, disgruntled employee, or even just an inexperienced staffer can cause untold trouble by misusing company checks. In the past, banks ate the losses associated with check fraud. This is no longer the case. They just can't afford these hits to their bottom line. Often, this area is overlooked—no one gives it much thought. However, with all the attention of the recent accounting scandals, the enactment of the Sarbanes-Oxley Act (S-Ox), and the new emphasis on internal controls, how a company stores its checks is likely to come under increased scrutiny. These procedures should be followed:

- Checks should be stored in a secure, locked location.
- Access to the check stock should be severely limited.
- The closet should be reinforced and not of the type that a crook could easily hack into.
- The lock on the door should be substantial and not easily picked with a hairpin or clothes hanger.

Ideally, the check storage closet should not be close to the printer. If someone breaks in, especially over a long weekend, don't make it too easy for the thief. Sufficient segregation of duties should be incorporated into the various tasks associated with the check production cycle, so the individuals with access to the check storage closet do not also have the authority to print checks. Clearly, anyone with access to the check storage closet should not be responsible for the reconciliation of the company's bank accounts.

CHECK PRINTING

Companies print checks as frequently as every day and as infrequently as once or twice a month, depending on numerous factors, which can include:

- Corporate culture
- Cash management practices
- Number of checks printed
- Check-signing practices
- Check-printing practices
- Efficiencies in the invoice handling procedures

As strange as it may seem, a few companies print checks only once or twice a month, not because that is an efficient way for them to run their business, but because they feel it gives them greater control over their cash flow. They can tell a vendor that they will print their check at the first opportunity, which will be in two or three weeks in the very next check run. Unfortunately for them, this excuse often ends up with the vendor threatening to put the company on credit hold, which in turn results in manual Rush (and very inefficient) checks. As those who are familiar with the implications of Rush checks are well aware, this can in turn lead to an increase in duplicate payments and potential fraud.

Obviously, the size of the company and the number of checks it needs to issue will directly affect the frequency of its check runs.

Some might argue that the best practice when it comes to printing checks would be to not print any checks at all, but rather to convert to a 100% electronic medium relying on the ACH. They would probably be right. At this time, however attractive that proposition might be, this is not a reasonable approach. Given that fact, we'll look at the state of check printing today.

Regardless of the type of printing used (mainframe or laser), all affected parties should be informed about not only what the check run schedule is but also the cutoff points. If an approved invoice or check request needs to be received in accounts payable by noon on Thursday in order to be included in a Friday check run, this vital information should be shared. Otherwise, people will show up in accounts payable on Friday morning with requests, expecting them to be included in that day's check run. In the long run, it is far better to spend the time communicating this information (verbally, in writing, and on the department's intranet site) with everyone who could possibly be affected.

WHO SHOULD PRINT CHECKS

The number of people who can print checks should be kept to a minimum. The person who prints the checks, usually by controlling the software (through user IDs and passwords), should not have access to the check stock. Theoretically, when using a laser printer (which, by the way, is regular laser printers), a check run can be made any time a manual check is requested. Each company must determine whether this approach is desirable and if it wishes to pursue that course.

When checks are printed this way, the process usually includes use of a facsimile signature. Typically, this signature is included on a separate plate. Companies take different stances about this plate—some leave them in the printer, whereas others remove them. If the plate is left in the printer (or is an integral part of the machine), additional care must be taken with the printer. It probably should not be left out on the open floor. Although in order to actually print a check someone would need access to the software and would need to have a password and user ID, a printer with a facsimile plate could turn a plain piece of paper into a negotiable check. (Remember, checks don't have to be printed on special safety paper, it's just a good idea.)

MONITORING CHECK STOCK USED

When preprinted check stock is used, a log similar to the one previously described should be kept. When it is time to run checks, one of the few approved staffers with access to the check stock closet should get the check stock out. Based on the number of checks that need to be run for each account, the appropriate number of checks should be removed. Some companies have so many different accounts that they end up using a cart to bring the appropriate number of checks for the different accounts to the computer room to be printed. The checks should not be stored close to the printer; it just makes it too easy for a thief. Typically, someone in the treasury or accounting departments will bring the checks up to the information technology (IT) department to be run. This representative should watch while the checks are printed.

Because this type of check is typically of a continuous format, it is difficult, if not impossible, to rerun a check (in the same check run) if something goes wrong. When the checks are printed, notations should be made in the log regarding the first check number, the last check number, and the number of checks printed. Both the representative from accounting (or treasury) and IT should initial the log.

If a check prints off center, jams, or has some other problem, it should be voided—either by writing VOID across the check in capital letters or by tearing off the magnetic ink character recognition (MICR) line. In any event, all damaged checks should be kept after voiding them to ensure that the checks are actually voided and do not land in the hands of a crook. Also, make sure the appropriate entries are made to your accounting logs, or it will look like an uncashed check that should be turned over to the state as unclaimed property.

Some companies like to have two people present when checks are printed regardless of the methodology. In this case, both people should calculate the number of checks used versus the check numbers and initial the log. Periodically, the log used to verify check counts versus check paper used should be audited—and occasionally on a surprise basis.

At regular intervals, say once every two years, or if there is any significant change in activity (e.g., due to a merger or spin-off), a review of the frequency of check runs should be undertaken. As part of this process, an analysis of the number of Rush checks (and the reasons for those requests) should be included. If too many Rush checks are required, a company may want to increase the frequency of its check-printing process. In the upcoming years, if electronic payments continue to increase, many midsize companies may be able to cut back on the number of check runs they have each month.

Anyone involved in the check-printing process should have no responsibility for reconciling the company's bank accounts.

BETWEEN PRINTING AND MAILING

Once the checks are printed, they should be kept with great care until they are mailed. This means that if they are not mailed the same day they are printed (as they ideally should be), they need to be kept in a secure location. They should not be kept on the credenza of an executive who has to provide a second signature or left lying around the accounts payable department. More than one sticky-fingered employee or cleaning person has walked off with a check that did not belong to him or her.

Yes, that means any time checks are waiting for signature or to be mailed, they should be locked back in that secure location where the check stock is stored. Companies that use laser

51

check stock and do not have a secure location as described earlier need to create a locked space where checks can be stored after printing and before they are mailed.

CHECK SIGNING

How checks are signed should depend largely on the upfront controls used to vet the invoice and the approval process. In reality there is a second component—corporate culture. In theory, if upfront controls for approvals and duplicate payment checking were perfect, there would be no need for a check to be signed by anything other than a machine. Very few companies, unfortunately, are in a position or are willing to let every payment fly through the invoice processing cycle without some level of senior executive checking for high-dollar invoices. The definition of high-dollar invoice varies from company to company.

The Board should authorize check signers. Alternatively, a senior-level executive who has been delegated by the Board may give others signatory responsibilities. In either event, banks will require signature cards so they can verify signatures on checks presented for payment. Do not assume from a bank's request for signature cards that it is checking signatures. *Banks do not verify signatures.* Occasionally, they will spot-check the signature on a check or pull a very large-dollar check to verify the signature. The emphasis here is on the word *occasionally.* Any company that is counting on its bank to catch fraudulent checks will find itself with a load of bad checks, unless it is using positive pay, which is discussed in Chapter 14.

Most companies put their top-level executives, such as the CEO, CFO, and so forth, on their bank accounts as signers, even though these individuals rarely sign checks. When these officers sign the annual report, they should *never* use their actual signature. This is for the company's protection and the protection of the officers personally. In the early days of check fraud, thieves simply got a copy of the company's annual report to get a legitimate signature to use in their crooked check activities. Because these executives rarely sign checks, it is recommended that they not be included as signers on bank accounts.

The selection of signers should depend on the number of checks that are manually signed as well as the personnel that will be available to actually sign the checks. Signers, however, should be of sufficient stature within the company and should check the documentation that accompanies the check for signature.

Most companies today use a mechanized check-signing procedure that is integrated with the check-printing cycle. Depending on the dollar amount of the check, the mechanized signature can be the only signature or the first signature. If a mechanized process is used, the signature plate needs to be maintained with proper care and controls. This means it should be either:

- Easily separated from the machine (computer) that prints the check

OR

- If it is not removed, the check-printing computer should be kept in a secure location, with controlled access.

The signature plate, or the machine with the plate in it, needs to be kept in a secure location with limited access. Many companies keep the signature plate used for facsimile signatures in a safe.

Even if upfront controls are airtight, most companies require two signatures on checks over a certain level. The level depends on the nature of the business and corporate culture. A smaller company might require the second signature for all checks over $25,000, whereas a Fortune 50 company might set that level at $1,000,000. The level reflects the company's comfort level with its invoice processing controls.

There is a lot of debate over whether a warning should be printed on the checks indicating the level where two signatures are required. This is similar to the warning regarding the maximum dollar amount that a check can be written for. Some feel that putting a notice on the check stating "checks over $25,000 require two signatures" is a good idea because it alerts the teller of a possible fraud. Others rightly note that such an indicator is likely to be of more use to a crook than to the teller. A crook noting such a warning will simply alter the check to no more than $24,999.

Most accounts payable and treasury groups at large companies keep a list of bank accounts and authorized signers. This is a good idea as long as proper care is kept with these reports. They should be limited in number and given only to those employees who need the information—definitely a need-to-know report. When the report is updated, the old reports should be collected and destroyed. Employees who receive the report should keep it inside their desks, not lying on top, for easy access.

In no case should anyone who is an authorized signer on any account do bank account reconciliations. When manual signatures are used on checks, the responsibility for getting the signatures should be given to someone other than the person who prepares the checks. When the check is given to the signer for signature, all of the appropriate backup should be attached, and the signer should verify that the:

- Check is actually for the invoices presented
- Appropriate approvals are in place
- Check is drawn on the correct account
- Check is for the correct amount

If the signer is not willing to or capable of completing this verification process, the person should not be an authorized signer.

Periodically, spot-check checks that are automatically signed to verify quality control.

DISTRIBUTION OF CHECKS

Once checks are printed and signed, they have to be put in the hands of the payee. The normal way this is handled is to mail the checks to the payee. In fact, some may wonder why there is a separate section for this topic. The answer is that sometimes the person requesting the check will request that the check be returned for final distribution. Typically, there are three semi-legitimate reasons this request is made:

1. The requestor wants to make sure that the check is mailed correctly.
2. The requestor is a salesperson who wants to deliver the check to the customer and try and pick up another order at the same time.
3. The requestor has some other business relationship with the payee and wants to solidify that relationship.

While the reasons may appear reasonable at first glance, they are overridden by several other concerns, including:

- It is extremely inefficient and time consuming to return checks to the requestor. Few people outside accounts payable realize how disruptive the practice is.
- The door for employee fraud is open wide whenever checks are returned to anyone other than the payee.
- Checks returned to the requestors are sometimes lost, misplaced, or not delivered for a long time, often resulting in duplicate payments.

MAILING CHECKS

When an invoice is approved for payment, the invoice should have a mailing address on it. Additionally, this address should match the Pay-To address in the master vendor file. Any variation from this should be investigated because it may be the first sign that something is amiss. Under all but the most extenuating circumstances, checks should be mailed. The section on check problems in this chapter provides a discussion of returning checks to requisitioners and the problems that can cause.

When checks are mailed, care should be taken regarding when and how this is done. Checks should be sealed in envelopes and delivered either straight to the post office or to the mailroom at the end of the day. If checks are delivered to the mailroom, they should not be left out in the open where anyone walking by can see them and easily take one. This is especially true if temporary employees are frequently employed.

Similarly, thought should be given as to whether a window envelope should be used. While window envelopes simplify the mailing of checks, they are also a red flag for a crook looking for checks to steal. Rarely are checks mailed in anything other than window envelopes.

Additionally, if one-part sealers (those multipart forms that contain the check) are used, extra care should be taken in the mailing procedures. Again, they are often a red flag to crooks looking for checks.

DIFFICULTIES CAUSED BY CHECKS

Checks can cause an inordinate number of headaches to those responsible for handling them. Even what seems to be a simple issue can cause massive problems and get you in trouble on the internal controls section of your Sarbanes-Oxley audit. The biggest problem, that of Rush checks, is discussed at length in the following chapter as it is an exception process.

While a move to electronic payments eliminates many of the problems encountered when paper checks are used, it is unlikely that paper checks will go the way of the dodo bird anytime soon. Hence, it becomes imperative that organizations what want to become as efficient as possible find ways to deal with the issues that paper checks inevitably bring with them.

WHY RETURNING CHECKS CAN BE A PROBLEM

Checks should not be returned to requestors for two simple reasons: (1) it's inefficient and (2) it opens the door to fraud. I could write a million words explaining the inconveniences to accounts payable caused by requests to return checks and it might make some impact on a few readers. I could write about the potential for fraud in theory and not make half the impact that one of our readers did with a real-life tale. Here is the story in the professional's words:

> A former employee, who was in charge of all the tradeshow planning, would request checks to be processed, payable to the tradeshows. The request was approved by the same person using the initials of their superior. This was common practice at that time, due to the lengthy traveling the superior does. Now when I think about it, how stupid were we to put that much trust in someone? We have a list of people allowed to sign the checks here, none are stamped. Those individuals signed these checks, trusting the former employee, and allowed me to return the checks to her believing they were getting sent to the tradeshows. Never in my wildest dreams did I ever imagine it was possible for a check made payable to another business to be allowed to be deposited into a personal bank account. Five years into the situation, one of the VPs decided to find out why the tradeshows were costing so much. We found out why. This ordeal cost the company a lot of money. Since then we have drastically changed our policies. *I will not give any check back to the requester.* The only exception to this rule is that a specific request must be signed off by an officer of the company.

This story emphasizes, once again, the old chestnut about fraud being committed by long-term trusted employees.

Readers should be aware that under Sarbanes-Oxley, returning checks to requisitioners could be considered poor internal controls.

AN END RUN AROUND THE RETURNING CHECK TO REQUISITION PROBLEM

Getting as many vendors as possible to set up for ACH payment helps. This way there is no check to return, and the confrontation with the requestor is avoided. Now some might point out that this does not address the underlying issue within the company, but it does avoid some of the battles and allows accounts payable to chip away at the problem, especially if management isn't willing to back a No-Return to Requisitioner Policy.

Here's another way to make ACH work for you in this regard: If certain employees routinely demand that checks be returned to them for certain vendors and management allows it, consider recruiting the vendor in question for participation in your ACH program. Once you have the vendor on board for ACH, you can even tell the requestor that the vendor prefers payment this way. By the way, given the earlier tradeshow example, this approach would have uncovered the fraud.

Check Processing Alternatives

As you can probably tell from the discussion so far, anything that gets rid of paper checks generally contributes to a smoother running operation. Additionally, there is a typically a cost savings associated with getting rid of the paper. When it comes to checks, the savings comes from several areas. These include:

- Purchase of the check stock
- Postage
- Check storage costs

- Check printing costs
- Check signing costs

Additionally—and this is a big one—there are no escheat problems. As most readers know, the states consider uncashed checks, unclaimed property. Under that classification, the value of the checks that remain uncashed are supposed to be turned over to the states at differing intervals of time. When electronic payments are used instead of paper checks, the problem goes away as there are no checks that remain uncashed.

Thus it is generally recommended that organizations looking to instill best practices embrace electronic payment methodology. Executives who use electronic payments in their personal lives are apt to encourage use at work as they have personally experienced the advantages. Although some drag their feet, once an organization gets started on this road, they typically go full throttle ahead.

Don't Overlook Corporate Credit Cards

Another way to eliminate checks is the corporate procurement card. A good number of organizations now use these handy tools to facilitate small dollar purchases. As we've discussed elsewhere, invoices are costly to process. Better to have your staff focus their time on the large dollar invoices where your organization has some exposure than to spend their time culling through $20 and $50 invoices.

Used properly, as discussed in more detail in Chapter 10, p-cards can make your accounts payable operation much more efficient. An added bonus, as many organizations are learning is the rebate, which actually puts money back in your pocket. Thus, the p-card not only saves you money by getting many of those small dollar invoices out of your accounts payable department, it also adds cash to your bottom line.

A Brief Discussion of Fraud

Interestingly, at least to this author, is the fact that the techniques used to minimize duplicate payments (which are discussed in Chapter 5) will also make check fraud (discussed in detail in Chapter 14) more difficult. The pertinent issue here is the legal implications from poor policies and internal controls and how that will affect your bottom line. The legal implications, as you will read in Chapter 14, call for you to exercise *ordinary care* when it comes to the handling of your checks before they are mailed.

To be blunt about it, ordinary care translates into using common sense when it comes to checks—not leaving them around where anyone can swipe one, storing unsigned checks under lock and key etc.

Impact on Accounts Payable

So, what exactly is meant by ordinary care when it comes to your disbursement practices? Now, if you are thinking that reasonable care means good, strong internal controls related to your check preparation and storage processes, you are on the right track, but you are only part of the way there. Your banker may consider not using positive pay not exercising ordinary care. Without a doubt, positive pay is one of the best steps a company can take to stop check fraud in its tracks. Every company should use it, but a significant number of companies still don't use it.

Some banks are so insistent that their customers use positive pay that they insert a statement in their deposit agreements that effectively places the liability for check fraud on their customers if the customer does not use positive pay. Accounts payable rarely sees the deposit agreements. Typically, the treasurer or controller will handle this document. If they are not sufficiently informed about the positive pay issue, this could slip past them.

Now, you may be wondering if this is legal. The UCC does not permit banks to simply disclaim their responsibility. However, the rules do not prevent parties from agreeing to shift liability from one party to another, and that is what your company has done if it accepts that depository agreement.

What Should You Do?

Use positive pay. It is simply the best safeguard your company has against check fraud. See the Positive Pay and Its Cousins section that follows for an explanation of positive pay and the enhancements that some banks have introduced to make the product stronger.

If your organization is not using positive pay, ask to see the deposit agreement to make sure that bank has not passed the liability on to your organization. Claiming ignorance will get you nowhere if a fraudulent check makes it through the system. Even if there is nothing in the deposit agreement, you might inquire from the treasurer, controller, or whoever is responsible for banking relationships if the firm ever signed a letter refusing to accept positive pay. Some banks require this and use it as a defense to shift payment responsibility to their customers in cases of check fraud. We've heard of several cases where the bank refused an account if the letter wasn't signed if positive pay wasn't used.

Check fraud is a fact of business life. No matter how careful an organization is, it happens. Virtually every company gets hit at one point or another. By knowing what the risks and alternatives are, you will be in the best position to limit your firm's exposure in case of check fraud.

POSITIVE PAY AND ITS COUSINS

Positive pay is a product banks use to help thwart check fraud. Virtually every check expert agrees that it is the best defense against check fraud. However, crooks are a resourceful lot, and just as quickly as the legitimate business world develops protection against their shifty ways, the fraudsters find ways to circumvent the safeguards. This is what has happened to some extent with positive pay and has led to some very interesting innovations as the corporate world tries to protect itself against check fraud.

Basic Model

The basic positive pay model requires that the company send a file to the bank each time it does a check run. The file contains check numbers and dollar amounts of all checks issued. The bank then matches all checks that come in for clearing against this file. Once a check comes in and is paid, the item is removed from the file and cannot be paid again.

This approach took a big whack at the check fraud problem. It eliminated several huge check fraud issues, including:

- The copying of one check numerous times and the subsequent cashing of all of them
- The altering of the dollar amount on a check
- The complete manufacture of fraudulent checks drawn on an organization's bank account

What the basic model did not address were checks cashed by tellers and checks where the payee's name was changed. Additionally, companies that could not produce a check-issued file for transmission to their banks were left unprotected. As might be expected, once the crooks got wind of positive pay, some adjusted their sights, focusing more on changing the payee's name rather than the dollar amount and on checks cashed at teller windows. But before we look at the products that address those issues, let's look at the banks' response for those companies that could not produce a check-issued file.

Reverse Positive Pay

Recognizing that not every organization was able or willing to produce the tape needed for positive pay, banks introduced another service. It's called reverse because it reverses the process. Each morning the bank tells the company what checks have been presented for clearing. It is up to the company to check those listings and make sure that they are all legitimate. Typically, there is a fallback position if the company does not notify the bank, and usually that is that the bank pays on the check. The action should be discussed with the bank when the reverse positive pay relationship is initially set up.

Teller Positive Pay

Once it became obvious that checks were being verified before they were honored, crooks realized that most tellers did not have this information and started cashing phony checks in person. Some banks now make this information available to their tellers on the platforms. If your bank is one such bank, ask how frequently this information is updated. Some update continuously, whereas others only update this information overnight. If it is only overnight, you could have some angry or annoyed vendors or employees on your hands if they try to cash checks you give them on the same day they are issued. A phone call usually takes care of these situations.

Payee Name Positive Pay

Recognizing that fraudsters were reduced to focusing their efforts on changing the payee names on checks, a few banks have taken up the fight in that regard. In addition to the check number and dollar amount, they will also verify the payee name. Will this completely stop check fraud? Probably not, but it certainly will make it more difficult for the crooks trying to separate your company from its funds.

P-CARDS

For lack of a better description, p-cards are credit cards for businesses. They are also referred to as corporate procurement cards and purchasing cards. They have been a boon to accounts payable departments looking to get small-dollar invoices out of their hair so the staff can devote the lion's share of its attention to large-dollar invoices that deserve their scrutiny. P-cards are so important in terms of accounts payable that we have devoted Chapter 10 to their proper use. Suffice it to say at this point that p-cards are a very worthwhile tool when it comes to payment alternatives and will be discussed in detail further in the book.

WIRE TRANSFERS

Traditionally, wire transfers were used for large-dollar payments. Often, but not always, these payments were for international payables. A wire transfer is a transaction that you initiate through your bank, authorizing it to wire funds from your account to another party. These transactions can be initiated over the phone or online. Today most banks require a confirmation from a second party at your company. This confirming party must be prearranged and gets calls regarding all wires initiated by phone. If the transaction is initiated online, the confirmation can be done online as well.

The trouble for accounts payable comes when wire transfers are initiated outside accounts payable. This happens at approximately 75% of all companies. The problem is compounded if both accounts payable and another part of the company both initiate wire transfers. The other party is typically, but not always, the Treasurer's department. The problem arises when accounts payable does not know of the wire and then subsequently pays an invoice for the same item, effectively making a duplicate payment.

Wire transfers are sometimes demanded by vendors who have not been paid on time. In extreme cases, they may insist on such a payment before releasing a new order. Wire transfers are fine, albeit expensive, if their use is integrated into the payment system so that the purchase order associated with the invoice being paid is canceled.

ACH PAYMENTS

ACH credits, and to a lesser extent debits, are making serious inroads into the corporate payment structure. Sometimes referred to as direct deposit, they are being used to replace paper checks in record numbers. The most common applications are direct deposit of payroll and social security payments.

WHAT EVERY COMPANY NEEDS TO KNOW TO AVOID MAKING PAYMENTS TO TERRORISTS

You don't need this publication to tell you that terrorists are a nasty bunch. Their actions speak louder than any printed words. What you may not know, however, is that sometimes terrorist groups trick regular companies, like your firm, into paying them money they then funnel into illicit activities. Now, if you are thinking, "Not us, we are very careful about who we pay, and we don't pay anyone with odd-sounding names," you may be in for a rude awakening. These sorts often pose as U.S. companies using common names that would never raise a red flag.

What follows is a synopsis of what you need to know and what you should be doing to avoid trouble.

Background

As most reading this are aware, the Office of Foreign Assets Control (OFAC) of the U.S. Department of the Treasury administers and enforces economic and trade sanctions based on U.S. foreign policy and national security goals against targeted foreign countries, terrorists, international narcotics traffickers, and those engaged in activities related to the proliferation of weapons of mass destruction.

Specifically, as these sanctions relate to corporations, companies are prohibited from making payments to what are referred to as Specially Designated Nationals and Blocked Persons. Companies are expected to verify that they are not making payments to these individuals. Similarly, the Department of State has its own list, albeit a much smaller one, of Foreign Terrorist Organizations (FTOs) that companies must also avoid paying. This list is currently comprised of 40 such organizations. Before checks are printed, they should be checked against the OFAC and FTO lists.

Where to Check

The OFAC list can be downloaded from the Internet at *www.treas.gov/offices/enforcement/ofac/sdn/*. The list is periodically updated, so you should check back regularly to update your list. The list is available in several formats, including CSV and XTML. Don't be taken aback when you first see the list. The original list is long, but once you have it, the periodic updates are not massive.

Information about FTOs along with a current listing can be found at *www.state.gov/s/ct/rls/fs/37191.htm*. Make sure to scroll down to the bottom of the page to get the list.

How P-Cards Help

Clearly, this is serious business. The beauty of making payments using a p-card is that the banks are scrupulous about running payments against the list. When you use your p-card, the bank takes care of this time-consuming task for you.

4

Exception Processing

Exception processing, especially when it comes to checks, is a land-mine area for accounts payable. Few outside the process understand the havoc that what seems like an innocuous request can cause. Similarly, they do not understand what all the fuss is about when they request that a check be returned to them rather than to the payee. Hopefully, by the time you finish this chapter, you'll understand why you should ban both of these practices in your organization. We'll also look at the issues surrounding petty cash boxes, which are fast going the way of the buggy whip.

CHECK PROBLEMS: EXCEPTION PROCESSING HEADS THE LIST

Recently, readers of *Accounts Payable Now & Tomorrow* were surveyed and asked to identify their biggest check problem. The results were astounding. Close to 80% of the respondents indicated issues related to exception processing caused them the biggest headaches.

Here are the check problems as they were ranked in the poll:

Rush checks	57%
Returning checks to requisitioner	21
Lost in the mail	10
Signers	4
T&E reimbursement by check instead of automated clearinghouse (ACH)	4
Casual handling by vendors	2
Other	2

TYPICAL RUSH CHECK SCENARIO

Here's a typical scenario that is likely to set off fireworks. The purchasing manager has forgotten to approve an invoice, and it is now 45 days past due. The vendor is fed up with the company because this is not the first time such an omission has happened. So the supplier tells the purchasing manager that unless a check is received within 24 hours, the next order will not be shipped.

The purchasing manager quickly scrawls his approval onto the invoice and runs down to accounts payable with the invoice hoping that he can get a check, which he'll either hand-deliver or send via express mail to the vendor so the organization is not put on credit hold. Do you see the problems that are about to unfold?

In our hypothetical example, the purchasing manager approaches the accounts payable manager for a check to be produced outside the normal production cycle and the accounts payable manager goes ballistic. To an outsider this seems unreasonable. What's the big deal? How long does it take to stop and write a check?

What the outsider who is looking askance at the accounts payable manager making the fuss does not understand is that this is the third time in the current week that the purchasing manager has been approached with a "special request." Additionally, the outsider does not realize the problems a check produced outside the check production cycle can cause. We'll address that issue in detail.

Finally, the outsider doesn't calculate the hit that the departmental productivity takes just because the purchasing manager in our example "forgets" to approve an invoice. If it takes 15 minutes to get the check book out, the check written and signed by an authorized signer, and the appropriate entries made to the accounting system and positive pay, that would not be too bad. If, however, you multiply this by 40 or 60 times that it may actually happen in a week, you begin to see the problem. The issue is so bad in some companies that a separate person has to be hired just to handle these emergencies. If they really were emergencies, which will happen, that would be one thing. But, more than 95% of the time, Rush check requests are simply a result of someone failing to do his or her job correctly. In fact, some accounts payable managers (not necessarily those interested in developing strong relationships with others) have a sign in their office that reads something like:

> A Failure to Do What You Were Supposed to Do Does Not Create an Emergency for Accounts Payable

BACKGROUND ON RUSH CHECKS

Rush checks, also referred to as emergency checks, priority checks, or ASAP checks, are the bane of many AP departments. They are traditionally manually written, although in recent years they have been printed by computers and are produced outside the normal check production cycle. They are supposed to be for those once-in-a-lifetime emergencies that crop up with varying frequency depending on the nature of the business and the tolerance of the corporation for this type of behavior. In reality, they are sometimes written to cover for the sloppy habits of certain employees, such as executives who get behind in their work and neglect to approve invoices for payment, harried purchasing managers who lose an invoice in the stacks of paper on their desks, or late-to-the-game employees who rush in an expense report the day their credit card bill is due.

While everyone realizes that there are true emergencies, and invoices occasionally do get lost in the mail, the practice of relying on accounts payable to bail out others for their poor work habits comes at a cost that is much higher than it appears. The hidden costs associated with these transactions include:

- The accounts payable associate must interrupt his or her work to process the request. If this happens more than very occasionally, an additional person will have to be added to the staff or overtime will be accrued.

- The person whose work was interrupted will have to find exactly where he or she was when work was stopped and continue. This increases the chances of an error being made that will have to be corrected at a later point.

- Manual checks will have to be entered into the system to get onto the company's books at a later point, taking more time. If the company is using positive pay, the check issuance file that is given to the bank has to be adjusted.

- Duplicate payment audit firms report that there is an increased risk for a duplicate payment anytime a check is written outside the normal cycle. The cost of recovering duplicate payments is huge.

There is one other consideration when it comes to Rush checks. There is also an increased risk of check fraud with Rush checks, especially if they are used often and the check issuance files given to the bank for positive pay are sloppily updated.

WAYS TO MINIMIZE THE NUMBER OF RUSH CHECKS

By now you probably realize that the best way to eliminate rush checks is to "just say no" and never issue checks outside the normal check production cycle. In most cases, this is not a realistic alternative because either management will not support this practice or it is not a practical business alternative. A more reasoned approach is to issue Rush checks occasionally under very strict guidelines. These might include requiring:

- Very-senior-level authorization so that the employees understand that it is a process for only true emergencies, and so management begins to understand the level of discomfort these transactions cause. More than one senior manager has reported that she thought accounts payable was making a big deal out of nothing regarding Rush checks. After having their work interrupted several times a day, senior managers often quickly change their opinion.

- The person making the request to get senior-level approval. This often makes the requestor think twice about whether the emergency is really an emergency.

- A thorough checking of the files before the Rush check is issued. Sometimes requestors find that the payment the vendor claimed it didn't receive was in fact deposited at the vendor's lockbox and the cash applied incorrectly.

- That accounts payable thoroughly question the requestor about the reasons for the rush request as well as the date when the payment must be made. Often, these requests are made out of ignorance about the actual accounts payable procedures, and with a little investigation it will turn out that the request can be handled through the normal cycle.

- That accounts payable keep a file with copies of all Rush check requests in it. Most times when a duplicate payment occurs that is related to a rush request and a lost invoice, the original invoice gets paid the second time, not the second request invoice. Eventually, the original invoice, whether it was lost in the mail or on someone's desk, finds its way to accounts payable and is paid. If the number of Rush checks issued is small, as it should be, the file will be thin. Once a month, an associate in the accounts payable department should check to ensure that the rush invoices were not paid a second time. If such a payment is discovered, the company can work with the supplier to recover the payment rather than paying its duplicate payment audit firm to handle the task.

Additional strategies can be used to reduce the number of Rush checks. They include:

- Make sure everyone who requests payments is aware of the check production schedule. This includes letting them know what the cutoff dates are for each check run.
- Periodically, review AP's procedures and its check run schedule to see if they have sufficient controls and are adequate to meet the company's needs.

POSITIVE PAY ISSUE

Checks issued outside the normal cycle have to be reincorporated into the positive pay reporting to your bank. If this step is forgotten, you can end up with egg on your face. After rushing around to get the vendor its check, the check may then be refused at the bank. It is important for any organization to incorporate positive pay reporting into its Rush check procedures.

WHY RETURNING CHECKS CAN BE A PROBLEM

Checks should not be returned to requestors for two simple reasons: (1) it's inefficient and (2) it opens the door to fraud. It will also get you dinged on your S-Ox audit because it signals weak internal controls. There are also practical considerations. More than occasionally, the check never gets mailed out to the vender. Then accounts payable gets a call wondering where payment is. When they research the matter and find out that the department that picked up the check forgot to mail out the check, it makes for an unhappy accounts payable staff and an even unhappier vendor.

NEED CHECKS RETURNED:
HERE'S A POLICY YOU CAN USE

One of the semi-legitimate reasons employees ask for a check to be returned to them is that they need to attach it to some other material. This may be a conference registration, a subscription form, or something like that. While we are loathe to recommend anything that will add to the administrative burden in accounts payable, this is one time when, alas, that is what we are going to do. Set up a process that allows employees to send along material that must be included with the check and then make it part of the check mailing process that these items be reattached to the check prior to the mailing.

You can also try talking to employees who want their checks returned to find out the reason behind these requests. Sometimes you will be able to suggest an acceptable alternative. For example, occasionally an executive needs a check to present to a charitable organization. We've all seen the televised events with the executive presenting a huge facsimile of a check. You can create a similar, albeit not so large, reproduction for your executives to use.

AUDIT POINT

Both returning checks to requisitioners and having an excessive number of Rush checks could get your accounts payable department written up in your annual audit. This is one of those times that, if applicable, you can hide behind Sarbanes-Oxley. Allowing either of these practices on anything more than a very occasional basis does not demonstrate strong internal controls.

PETTY CASH BOX

Anecdotal evidence suggests that about 25% of all companies still have petty cash boxes. They are an invitation to trouble, so unless you absolutely must have one, get rid of it. More than a few companies handle their petty cash boxes in a cavalier manner—so many, in fact, that virtually everyone associated with the function has a horror story or two to tell.

Embezzlements that began as short-term loans, funds used to pay for activities that most would consider questionable at best, and personal IOUs form just the tip of the iceberg. My personal favorite relates to the fellow who had a fatal heart attack, leaving behind an IOU in the company petty cash box. This was all the ammunition the accounts payable manager needed to put an end to the practice of executives "borrowing" from the petty cash box.

A company that wants a well-run petty cash process should prohibit:

- Borrowing by any individual
- Check-cashing privileges for employees
- Access by anyone other than the individuals responsible for the box
- Unapproved cash disbursements

Additionally, studies should be undertaken periodically to determine the types of expenditures being made from the box. With this information in hand, steps should be taken to identify alternative methods of funding those expenditures. Here are a few that might work:

- Have the employee put the expenditure on a purchase card

- Have an employee pay for the item and request reimbursement through the T&E system
- Arrange to have the company billed for the item, especially if there are numerous disbursements for the same item
- Analyze whether the expenditures are really something the organization should be paying for
- Look into bulk purchases if appropriate

5

Duplicate and Erroneous Payments

Duplicate payments are, unfortunately, a fact of life in the corporate world. It is unlikely that they will ever be completely eliminated, but they can be minimized. Now if you are scratching your head over this statement, consider the following situations (all of which increase the likelihood of a duplicate payment):

- Invoices sit on an approver's desk for weeks while the approver focuses on everything but reviewing invoices.
- Companies decide to stretch terms, and the supplier sends a second invoice because it did not get paid.
- Invoices are actually lost in the mail.
- Priority (Rush or ASAP) or manual checks are used.
- Fraud, both at the vendor and employee level, is perpetrated.
- Disputes are not resolved in a timely manner.

79

These are just a few of the practices that allow a duplicate payment to slip through the cracks.

THE WE-NEVER-MAKE-A-DUPLICATE-PAYMENT MYTH

An unfortunate part of the duplicate payment issue is the large number of companies that truly believe they never make a duplicate payment. While these companies' processes may be first class, vendors play games and mistakes happen. Not only that, but fraud is a fact of corporate life, and the crooks who perpetrate invoice fraud know about duplicate payment checks and how to circumvent the controls put in place to thwart them.

Companies that believe they never make duplicate payments are often reluctant to bring in a duplicate payment audit firm. This is false vanity. Another reason some companies object to duplicate payment audit firms is that they think this service is too expensive. However, because most of these firms work on an incentive basis, earning a percentage of what they find, bringing one in costs nothing. With an audit firm, at least the company collects a percentage of the duplicate payment; without it, the company collects nothing.

DUPLICATE-PAYMENT HYPOCRISY

When asked how they guard against duplicate payments, a few controllers will tell you that they rely on "the memory of the clerk in accounts payable" to ensure that no duplicates are made. This is outrageous on so many levels. First, to expect any person to remember all the payments made by a company is not realistic, especially if the duplicate request floats in several months after the first one. Second, expecting someone in a clerk's position to have this kind of memory is unrealistic.

While some of the people who work in accounts payable are very good at remembering past payments (and these people

80

are worth their weight in gold to the organizations that hire them), they should just be your first line of defense against duplicates, not your entire army.

POLICY

Even those organizations that piously claim they never make a duplicate payment have them. There are just too many ways these payments can get made. Like the person who says he or she never makes a mistake, this claim does not stand up under the harsh light of day.

The realistic goal of any accounts payable organization when it comes to duplicate payments should be threefold:

1. *Prevention.* Don't make any duplicate payments.
2. *Identification.* Since we know that is unlikely, the secondary position should be to identify duplicates and erroneous payments before they go out the door.
3. *Reclamation.* Should the secondary goal fail, as it occasionally will, identify the dups after the fact and reclaim those funds.

Duplicate payments prevention, identification, and reclamation after the fact if a duplicate is made are the three prongs of a defense for best-practice accounts payable departments. So, how does this work?

Step 1: Include a rigorous checking routine before payments leave the company.

Step 2: Use third-party software or routines developed in-house (using Excel and/or Access) to do your own checking.

Step 3: After the fact, hire a duplicate payment audit firm to find those payments that managed to slip through.

IN-HOUSE CHECKING: BEFORE THE PAYMENT IS MADE

Companies employ all sorts of upfront checking to ensure that duplicate payments don't get made. Here are a few checks that might work in your organization:

- Establish a policy when paying from copies rather than original invoices. These procedures should include flagging payments made from copies and invoices over 30 days old.
- Require high-level approval for each payment requested from a copy and pay only after a thorough search has been made of the paid invoice file. It's amazing how many people manage to find the original invoice when this additional hurdle is added.
- Maintain a log of all prepayments and deposits. Additionally, a copy of the contract or agreement should be kept in the paid invoice file. Managers should regularly review the payment history of those vendors that require prepayments.
- Cross reference payments between entities. One of the easiest ways for a duplicate payment to slip through is to have one of the payments made to a related entity.
- Check the files to ensure payments have not been made for invoices over a certain threshold amount. That level will vary from organization to organization and should be set at a number that is deemed to be large for the firm. For some this may be every payment over $10,000 and for others it may be payments over $50,000.

IN-HOUSE CHECKING: AFTER THE PAYMENT IS MADE

Most accounts payable professionals know who their problem customers are. They also know which ones are likely to receive duplicate payments. Prepare a list of such vendors. Then, ask the IT department to run three reports by vendor. These reports should show payments made to each vendor by:

- Invoice number
- Dollar amount
- Invoice date

A manual review of these reports will allow the accounts payable department to identify those payments that should be investigated further. While this research is being done, collect all backup as to why the duplicate payment was made. Use this to identify root causes—and then fix them!

A WORD ABOUT SOFTWARE

The previous example shows how software can play a role in preventing duplicate payments. Today, many of the accounting packages have duplicate payment checking modules that can be run before the payments are released. These handy programs can identify potential duplicates before the money leaves your company. By finding the funds ahead of time, you also save the money that would have had to be paid to the duplicate payment audit firm that recovered the money later on. Unfortunately, many companies do not even realize they have this capability within their accounting software. Others know they have it but choose not to activate the module. It is a good idea to use these programs, if available.

If your software does not contain a duplicate payment checking module or you have chosen not to activate it, all is not lost. You can purchase third-party software or you can have your Excel and/or Access expert develop a routine that you run with every single check run to identify potential duplicates. You will note that we continue to refer to potential duplicates. Once the program had identified possible duplicate payments, one of your processors will have to investigate to see if the payment is indeed a duplicate. The beauty of software is that it can do rote checking quickly and permit your processors to focus on more value-added work.

One last comment is called for: The software discussed should not be relied on to completely stop all duplicate payments. It is simply one weapon in your arsenal to fight against this common problem.

WHY DUPLICATE PAYMENT AUDIT FIRMS ARE NEEDED

The last line of attack against duplicate payments is third-party audit firms. Now some controllers and CFOs think that if they make a duplicate payment, the vendor will return it. A *few* will, but the emphasis here is on the word few. Most won't. They either don't realize it is a duplicate or don't care.

The reality is that when a check comes in and it can't be applied, most companies simply deposit it and record it in a suspense account to be researched at a later date. Researching unapplied cash is a low priority in most organizations, especially when it is difficult to figure out what is going on. Eventually, these duplicates end up as credits on the vendor's books. In theory, these credits should eventually be turned over to the state, although many vendors don't do that either. They simply write off the amount to miscellaneous cash.

In actuality, vendors returning duplicate payments without being prompted by the customer are a rarity. Anecdotal evidence suggests that these returns are less than 1%. Hence, an alternative mechanism is needed to find those funds that were paid in error, and that is where duplicate payment audit firms come into the picture.

HIRING A POSTAUDIT FIRM

Most good duplicate payment audit firms, also referred to as postaudit firms or recovery audit firms, will work on a contingency basis. The ones that preferred to work on an hourly rate had difficulty competing, as few companies were willing to pay for the work without a guarantee that the firms would find anything.

While most firms do not talk publicly about their rates, anecdotal evidence suggests that rates have dropped from about 33% a few years ago to 25% and even lower in recent times. This has made life a little tougher for these firms. Also, companies that are tired of paying others to find money they could easily find themselves had been setting up their own in-house recovery units. This is not to say that they are not using these firms, but rather that they are finding the easier reclamations themselves first, leaving the more difficult recoveries to the postaudit firms.

When interviewing potential audit firms to handle your audit, focus on the following areas:

- The minimum dollar amount that they will recover (this is especially important if you have lots of small-dollar payments).
- The firm's experience in your industry. Someone with lots of experience with your vendors will know where duplicates are likely to be made.
- How the recovery will be made and how the audit firm will be paid in relation to that recovery.
- Technology requirements.
- Confidentiality issues (most companies do not want to advertise that they use a duplicate payment recovery firm).
- Whether you will get a report afterward identifying weaknesses in your process that can be closed so future duplicates do not occur.
- Get references, but check them with a grain of salt. Only the lamest of firms will give you a reference that will not be glowing.

There is a big debate among the audit firms over the way their auditors are compensated. This is a hotly contested issue, with each side feeling passionately that its way will get the best results for customers. Some pay a straight salary and small commission, whereas others pay almost 100% contingency.

To find a list of such firms, go to *http://directory.google.com/ Top/Business/Accounting/Business-to-Business/Recovery_Audit/*.

SECOND POSTAUDIT

Depending on the size of your payables and the recovery made during your primary audit, you might want to consider having a second audit done. The reason for this is that each firm has its own proprietary methods for finding duplicates. While they all will request statements to find those unused credits, their techniques diverge after that. Thus, many organizations routinely have two audits.

If you do this, it is only fair to disclose that the audit is a secondary one. Many firms are happy to do this for two reasons. First, they realize that if they do a spectacular job, you are likely to hire them for the primary audit in the following year. The second reason is financial. The recovery rates demanded for secondary audits may be as high as 50%. The reason for this is that they are not likely to recover nearly as much as the primary auditor did. Many companies routinely have a second audit. After all, it doesn't cost anything.

Occasionally, two audit firms will use very similar methods for recovery. If you hire one of these organizations, they will not find much. That is another reason why you should tell them that it is a secondary audit. After a while, they know which firms have similar techniques and will not be interested in doing a secondary after those firms. They will not share this information with you but will either not bid or bid at a very high rate.

WORD OF CAUTION

Many accounts payable professionals get nervous when they hear their organization is bringing in a third-party auditor to look for duplicate payments. This is because in more than a few organizations they will be blamed for the duplicate. This censure is not always fair. If a company refuses to use the duplicate payment checking module, allows numerous Rush checks, and approvers routinely approve duplicate invoices, duplicate payments will occur. Professionals in the audit field report that less than one-quarter of the duplicate payments they find are a result of mistakes made in accounts payable.

We share this information to suggest that if you hire a duplicate payment firm and it finds a significant amount of money, ask it to identify the loopholes that allowed these payments to happen in the first place. With this information in hand, you can tighten the weak points and identify the true culprits, who may or may not be in accounts payable. The purchasing executive who leaves invoices sit unapproved for weeks on end plays a leading role in the resulting duplicates that occur.

OVERALL ACTION PLAN

Once you have taken the first step of recognizing that there is a problem, you are ready to implement a comprehensive action plan to eliminate the problem. What follows are 13 steps you can take to accomplish this goal:

Step 1: Use coding standards for both your master vendor file and Invoice data entry to minimize the chance of an invoice slipping through a second time.

Step 2: Eliminate duplicate vendors from your master vendor file. Once you have identified a duplicate vendor, make sure the data gets merged with the file that will remain. You do not want to lose any supplier payment history.

Step 3: Do everything possible to eliminate the need for the supplier to send a second invoice. This includes paying at or near term and keeping the vendor informed of any change to your standard terms.

Step 4: Check records for any payment over $50,000 before releasing the check. The $50,000 number is not set in stone and should be adjusted to a level appropriate for each organization.

Step 5: Before releasing checks, run a list of the dollar amounts of all checks issued in the prior 90 days and check for any duplicate amounts. If multiple invoices are paid with one check, this approach is less likely to spot duplicates.

Step 6: Keep track of every invoice that enters accounts payable, including disputed invoices. Never just send an invoice back to purchasing for reconciliation with a supplier without entering it on a log so you can answer any inquiries about it. This helps prevent the vendor from sending a second invoice.

Step 7: Once you have located duplicate payments, keep track of the root causes. Periodically, say quarterly, analyze all of your potential duplicates and try to eliminate the problem areas that are generating the most duplicates.

Step 8: If your organization installs a new accounting system or goes through a system upgrade, take special care in searching for potential duplicates. If an invoice shows up for payment dated prior to the system switchover, check the old system to see if the payment was made.

Step 9: Occasionally, vendors will change the invoice number on second copies of invoices. This may be something as simple as adding a letter at the end of the invoice number or something more insidious. Whether this is done for a less than honest reason is irrelevant. It will wreck havoc with your duplicate payment tracking processes that depend on the invoice number, as most do. Keep a list of such vendors and double-check all of their invoices when processing for payment.

Step 10: Periodically cleanse your vendor file. Ideally, this should be done quarterly, but most organizations manage to get it done annually. Any vendor that has had no activity for the prior 12 months should be deactivated. Do not delete the vendor because you will lose the payment history. This information can be important if the supplier claims nonpayment.

Step 11: Never pay from a statement unless an arrangement has been made with a supplier to only pay from statements. You might do this with vendors who submit many small-dollar invoices throughout the month. If you employ such a practice, it should be an all-or-nothing affair. Also, your system should be flagged to prevent invoices from being processed for this vendor.

Step 12: Request statements from all vendors at least annually. The letter should emphatically state that you want vendors to include all activity, including open credits. A good portion of credits are duplicate payments. You can either request that a check be issued for those credits (this is my preference because it keeps a clean audit trail) or take those credits against future invoices. Also use these statements to identify older invoices that have not made their way into accounts payable. Do not pay from the statement.

Step 13: Periodically, say once a year, hire a duplicate payment audit firm to search for duplicates that managed to slip through your almost iron-clad system.

Duplicate and erroneous payments are a very serious issue. If your organization has never had a review by one of the postaudit recovery firms, you should probably do so. Although they don't find as much as they used to at those companies that have aggressive programs for identifying duplicates before the fact, there is a place for them in the corporate structure. If you think duplicate payments are not made in your organization, you have nothing to lose; hire one of the firms that works on a contingency basis. If you are correct, the exercise will cost you nothing, but if you are wrong . . .

6

Vendors, Vendor Relations, and Master Vendor File

While at first glance vendor relations appears to be a purchasing topic and not an accounts payable issue, that is not the case. Yes, vendor relations need to be handled through purchasing, but if the payment component is ignored, relations with vendors can become tarnished quickly. Sometimes, as you have read in this book, accounts payable becomes the scapegoat for problems that occur other places in the procure-to-pay cycle. By including the payment piece in discussions with vendors, the entire cycle will operate more smoothly, and that inclusion means making sure that the promises made to vendors can be honored by the accounts payable department.

VENDOR RELATIONS

It makes no sense to promise a vendor payment within X days if it takes your organization X plus seven days to turn around an invoice. This is just begging for trouble with your suppliers. By giving the supplier a realistic idea of how you will be able to pay their invoices, you are setting the groundwork for good vendor relations.

More than one purchasing initiative has faltered because no attention was given to the payment end of things. One high-flying e-commerce initiative fell apart when accounts payable was completely left out of the discussions. After spending $1 million to create an e-commerce initiative for purchasing, this organization devoted one sentence to the payment focus. This is what the documentation said, "the payment will be made." If only a fraction of the attention given to the rest of the process had been focused on the payment piece, the project might have been a success. Unfortunately, this project fell apart and the company lost its entire investment.

WHAT IS THE MASTER VENDOR FILE?

The master vendor file is the repository of information for all vendors with whom the company does business. Not just any vendor should be able to get into your master vendor file. Before a vendor is entered, information should be checked verifying that the vendor is legitimate and that your organization intends to do business with it. Generally speaking, most organizations do not enter one-time vendors into their master vendor file. Controls around the information, both the initial data and any changes, should be strong.

RESPONSIBILITY FOR THE MASTER VENDOR FILE

The ownership of the master vendor file typically lies either in purchasing or in accounts payable. While an argument can be made for either, the balance tips in favor of accounts payable because accounts payable does not generally approve invoices for payment. Additionally, they do not select vendors.

In addition to ownership of the file, the question of access has to be addressed. While the number of people who can look

92

at the information in the file may be large, those who can actually make changes should be limited to a handful. These changes should only be made if sanctioned by someone who is authorized to do so.

WHO'S IN AND WHO'S NOT?

One of the biggest issues to be addressed is when to add a vendor to the master vendor file. The best functionality can be obtained from your master vendor file if only those vendors that are used regularly are allocated a spot. It should be noted that some systems cannot generate a payment unless the vendor is in the master vendor file. In that case, each vendor must be added.

Generally speaking, however, one-time vendors should not be added. They simply clutter the files, opening the door to employee error and fraud. A good rule of thumb is to put vendors in the active file if they receive payments at least three times a year. Of course, depending on your business requirements, this number may be increased.

HANDLING INACTIVE VENDORS

As business requirements change, a vendor may no longer be used. Periodically—and at least annually—all entries in the master vendor file should be reviewed to determine whether they should be deactivated. Some professionals talk about purging the master vendor file; this position needs to be clarified. The master vendor file should be purged of inactive vendors, but that information should be retained for future reference. Hence, many systems let you deactivate vendors, which is the recommended procedure.

If inactive vendors must be removed from your system, make sure the data related to all past activity is retained. This is crucial for your duplicate payment auditors, who are looking for excess payments, as well as to reply to any inquiries your vendors may have in the future.

Finally, if you are employing the best practice of periodically requesting vendor statements to identify unapplied credits, you will need your past history to back up any claims and refute any allegations the vendor may make.

CLEANSING THE MASTER VENDOR FILE

Periodically, the master vendor file should be reviewed. Most organizations do this annually, but quarterly is not a bad idea, either. As a general rule of thumb, all vendors who have not had any activity within the last 13 months should be inactivated. This prevents unscrupulous employees from passing an invoice through that inactive account. The vendor history should be maintained in case of disputes later on.

Readers should also be aware that some companies completely ignore this task, never cleansing (or purging) these files. This is a really bad practice because it makes it easy for shifty employees to play games.

FRAUD THROUGH THE MASTER VENDOR FILE

We have mentioned fraud using the master vendor file several times now, and you may be wondering how this can be done. Needless to say, your employees with larceny in their hearts can probably find more ways to play games than we can identify. We'll hone in on a few of the easier scams.

The most common vendor master file game is to simply submit a phony invoice (usually for a small dollar amount) for payment. If your controls are weak and someone approves the phony invoice because he or she is rushed, the vendor has then attained "legitimacy," and then future phony invoices, perhaps for larger dollar amounts, can slip through.

More devious employees have been known to hone in on inactive vendors that are still live in the master vendor file. They then submit an invoice under that vendor's name and address. Now, here comes the tricky part. Once the invoice has been approved for payment, the thieving employee goes into the master vendor file and changes the Remit To address to their own address or that of an accomplice. Once they have the check in hand, they go back to the master vendor file and change the Remit To address back to the original address.

These same tricks can be used to divert payments from a legitimate vendor to your dishonest employee. This is why in the Access to the Master Vendor File and Making Changes section, you will see that we harp on controls around the master vendor file.

VENDOR WELCOME LETTER

One of the best ways to ensure that you and the vendor are on the same page is to send a vendor welcome letter. In this communiqué, the vendor should be given instructions on what has to be done in order to get paid on time. This should include an honest explanation of what your terms are. If your terms are 60 days, disclose this in your welcome letter. Note: Purchasing should have divulged this in the negotiations. It really should not come as a surprise to the vendor.

The vendor should also be told where to send the invoices. Some prefer to have all invoices sent to accounts payable, whereas others have all invoices sent to the purchaser. In any event, all invoices should, at a minimum, contain the name of the purchaser and/or the purchase order number.

Letters of this sort can be sent any time there is a change that will affect the vendors (e.g., if there is a change in mailing address). Alternatively, if a letter has never been sent to vendors, it might not be a bad idea to send one, especially if invoices are sent all over the place and not to one location.

NEW VENDOR APPLICATIONS

Just because an invoice shows up, the vendor in question should not necessarily be entered into your master vendor file. That's how crooks get onto your payroll. Before you start to do business with a particular vendor, supply them with a vendor application. This form does not have to be lengthy. It should require that the vendor provide you with enough information so a party within your organization, but not the sponsoring executive, can verify the vendor as legitimate. Here's a list of some of the pieces of information you might require:

- Legal name
- DBA (doing business as) name(s)
- Mailing address
- Remit to address
- Phone number (main)
- Fax number (main)
- Web site address
- Contact name
- Contact e-mail address
- Contact phone number
- Brief explanation of company's line of business
- W-9 (signed)

This information should be verified separately. For example, do not use the phone number provided on the application to verify that the entity is in business. Look the number up in the phone book and call to verify. Alternatively, call directory assistance and ask for the phone number.

You might also ask for some of the following information if it is important to your firm:

- Is the vendor a small business?
- Is the vendor a woman-owned business?

- Is the vendor a minority-owned business?
- If you are going to pay electronically, request the appropriate banking information.
- Other special industry-specific information.

Because this application contains some sensitive information, it is imperative that access be limited on a need-to-know basis. It is a good idea, if possible, to severely limit access to the taxpayer identification numbers (TINs) and banking information. This is as much for the protection of your company as it is for the protection of sensitive vendor information.

ACCESS TO THE MASTER VENDOR FILE AND MAKING CHANGES

Certain information in the master vendor file should be shielded from all but a few individuals. Your invoice processors will need to check the master vendor files when processing invoices, as will your purchasing professionals. However, neither group needs access to the banking or TIN information.

From time to time, information related to your vendors will change. They will move, your primary contacts will change, or the vendors will change banks, requiring a change in the banking information in your files. Changes to this information should require that:

- A special form be filled out and any backup and/or explanation attached.
- The form be signed by one person within the company.
- The form be approved by a second person at a higher level.
- The form is then forwarded to the master vendor file person, who enters the information.

When the information has been entered, the original requestor should be informed.

REVIEW OF CHANGES

Making changes to the master vendor file is one way sneaky employees commit fraud. It is why the next step is recommended, even though it may seem somewhat tedious and perhaps overkill. Periodically, depending on the volume of changes, a report should be run detailing all of the changes made to the master vendor file. This report should be given to a fairly high-level employee, who reviews each of the entries in the report to detect any unusual activity. The fact that this report is run and given to a high-level employee, say the controller, should be well publicized within the company.

I realize that this is not a task that would normally be done by the controller or CFO. However, by widely publicizing the fact that this review is being done at this level, the process also deters those who are contemplating playing games with the file. If the controller or CFO is simply not willing to undertake this review, try running a shorter report just showing changes to the Remit To address for the controller/CFO review.

THE SPOT-CHECK ANNUAL REVIEW

A second step should be undertaken periodically. Perhaps once a year, run a report by vendor of all changes made to the master vendor file. Even though the report is run once a year, have it cover the prior 15 months of activity. Review the activity by vendor. What should pop out here are any vendors with more than one change to the Remit To address. Additionally, look with special concern at changes made on inactive vendors.

While you are running this annual profile, you might also want to run a report matching all of your employees' addresses against the addresses in your master vendor file. This is another way to catch employees who are playing games with your master vendor file. While occasionally there may be a legitimate reason for a duplicate address, all such instances should be carefully investigated.

MASTER VENDOR FILE STANDARDS

One of the problems with master vendor files is that sometimes a vendor gets into the master vendor file more than one time. This allows duplicate payments to slip through. The master vendor file should be purged of these duplicates. This purging needs to be done carefully. Before the entry is purged, the activity needs to be merged into the remaining entry in the file.

While purging may get rid of the duplicate, a better approach is to avoid the problem altogether. By ensuring that a vendor only gets into the file once, the issue is avoided. Typically, vendors get into the file more than once because different processors enter vendor names differently. This brings up the issue of standards.

Some of the commentary that follows related to coding standards may seem like overkill. However, remember that without these standards, companies end up with numerous entries in the master vendor file for the same vendor, and that makes it possible for a duplicate payment to slip through.

CODING STANDARDS

Rigorous requirements related to the master vendor file should extend to the way vendors are set up in the file. Otherwise, you can very easily end up with duplicate entries for the same vendor, which greatly increases your chances of making a duplicate payment. It also makes year-end 1099 reporting a bit of a challenge. Therefore, we strongly recommend you employ a coding standard when entering vendors into the master vendor file. To make this process work most efficiently, the coding standard used should mirror the one used for invoice coding, at least as it relates to the vendor name.

If this seems like we are recommending an action that is too controlling, let's look at a simple example. The most frequently used company in this regard is IBM, because it demonstrates what can go wrong if a coding standard is not used.

IBM could be entered as:

- International Business Machine
- IBM
- IBM Corp.
- International Business Machines Corporation
- International Business Machine Corporation
- I.B.M.
- I B M

And, you can probably come up with additional variations. This is only a sampling of what can go wrong. Other problem issues include:

- Leading articles such as the, a, etc.
- Punctuation in a name (periods, apostrophes hyphens, and commas)
- Special characters (&, .com, etc.)
- In business names, including Inc., LLC, LLP, Corp., etc.
- In individual names, including titles such as Dr., Mr. etc.
- How you handle periods (.) in names
- How you handle DBAs (doing business as)
- How you handle numbers in names
- How you handle numbers in names (usually years) that change
- If you leave spaces between initials (i.e., IBM or I B M)
- How you handle individuals' names (i.e., Mary Jones or Jones, Mary)

Remember, the coding standard used for the master vendor file should mirror the part of your invoice coding standard that relates to vendor name.

COORDINATION WITH INVOICE CODING STANDARDS

To make your standards work, your processors should enter vendors' names from invoices using the same rules as when the vendor is set up in the master vendor file. Otherwise, your processor will not find the vendor and will attempt to have a new vendor set up in the file, which will delay processing. Have the standards coordinated for entering invoices and setting up vendors in the master vendor file.

VENDOR CALLS INTO ACCOUNTS PAYABLE

The first place that feels the effects of poor or insufficient vendor communications is the accounts payable department, specifically, the person charged with answering and researching vendor inquiries. Most of these calls are from suppliers looking for funds. They usually want to know the following:

- Why they haven't been paid yet
- When they are going to be paid
- Why there were deductions taken on the payment they did receive

These phone calls are disruptive and do not add value to the work produced in accounts payable. So, anything that can be done to minimize them will increase the efficiency of your accounts payable department. Additionally, as you may have already guessed, the tone of the conversations, given the subject matter, can occasionally be less than cordial. The process of having one or more employees find payment information for vendors can be time consuming.

IVR/IWR

If there were some way that the vendor could check this information themselves, it would not only reduce the stress in accounts payable, but it would also save some personnel costs and perhaps improve vendor relations. Now there is a way. It began with what is referred to as interactive voice recognition (IVR). These programs are similar to the type that are now commonly used by pharmacies for prescription refills.

The IVR systems permitted the vendor to use the keypad on their phones to retrieve information related to the payment of an outstanding invoice. By using certain passwords, vendors were able to find out the status of their invoices without having to chase personnel in accounts payable.

The Internet took this process a giant step forward. Now the information can be obtained online by companies that have chosen to implement what is referred to as interactive Web response (IWR). The IWR systems take the information another step, often alerting the vendor to where their invoice stands in the process. Thus, the vendor knows that the invoice, for example, is in purchasing waiting for approval. This alerts them to the proper person to question as to the holdup.

As you might imagine, accounts payable departments love this technology because it ends much of the game playing that went on in the past. The IWR systems have largely ended the installation of new IVR systems. However, many companies that had put in IVRs kept them because their vendors like them. Additionally, even when these companies have moved to IWR, some keep the IVR because the cost to keep it running is minimal.

Readers should also be aware that many of the new electronic invoicing programs have a vendor inquiry component that for all intents and purposes is an IWR. The most sophisticated of these systems also have an online dispute resolution feature built into them.

SEGREGATION OF DUTIES

Rarely does the issue of master vendor file surface when there is a discussion of segregation of duties. However, it is something that should be considered. A few duties should be segregated from the personnel responsible for entering information into the master vendor file. The person who is responsible for the master vendor file should not:

- Be an authorized signer
- Be able to approve invoices for payment
- Handle unclaimed property

CONTRACT COMPLIANCE

As accounts payable departments become more advanced and they spend less time doing rote data-entry work, contract compliance is becoming an issue. It is one of the last places that companies have to look to squeeze out productivity enhancements. With duplicate payment prevention and avoidance now almost under control, companies are turning their attention to one of the last unchallenged territories—that of contract compliance.

While the task of making sure what's on the invoice is what was in the contract originally signed by the company may sound simple, it is far from that. Contract compliance is an area where your staff can find additional savings for your organization. This assumes that:

- Accounts payable is given the contracts.
- Accounts payable is given adequate staff to monitor the contract.
- Accounts payable is given the authority to negotiate changes in the invoice if it finds pricing (or terms) that is not consistent with the signed contract.

Depending on the nature of your business, this may be a very complicated task. Hospitals, with their large inventory of supplies purchased from different vendors, are an example of an organization that would benefit from a contract compliance initiative.

To be perfectly honest, not everyone is putting their contract compliance unit in accounts payable. Some have it as a complete stand-alone unit and others have it as part of purchasing. It all depends on the corporate culture, staffing initiatives, and whether this is something the business needs. What is not realistic is to expect an already overworked accounts payable staff to take on any serious work related to contract compliance. However, if you've started using some new technology and approaches that have streamlined the accounts payable process, contract compliance might be a good task to have some of your better processors work on.

7

Discounts and Deductions

Discounts and deductions impact an organization's bottom line. Handled incorrectly, as they often are, they insidiously eat away at the organization's profitability in the form of productivity losses as the staff struggles to handle the fallout from the bad practices or the inappropriate application of policies, especially when it comes to early-payment discounts. These issues are among the few that might be deemed as part of the organization's financial planning.

LOST EARLY-PAYMENT DISCOUNTS

With interest rates so low, few CFOs or controllers would turn their noses up at an investment that returns 36% a year. In fact, most would actively pursue one that returned just half that. Yet, that is what thousands of organizations do when they allow inefficient processes to stand in the way of their firms earning those very attractive returns. What are we talking about?

Many, but certainly not all, vendors offer a financial incentive to entice their customers to pay early. The most common enticement is the 2/10 net 30 payment terms. As most reading this are well aware, this means that although the payment is due on the 30th day, a customer can take a 2% discount if it pays before the 10th day. While the individual amounts may seem small, they do add up. Losing a 2% discount on a $10,000 invoice may only result in $200 not earned, but multiply that by the number of invoices processed and the amounts start to add up.

Any introductory finance book will walk you through the math that demonstrates that 2/10 net 30 is equivalent to a 36% rate of return; hence even 1/10 net 30 translates into an 18% rate of return. Few companies can afford to look such gifts in the face, and that is precisely what those returns are.

This issue becomes even more crucial for companies operating on razor-thin margins because this extra return can make a huge difference in the bottom line. Yet, many organizations have such cumbersome and inefficient processes that it is impossible to get the invoice turned around in the requisite 10 days.

Now, if you are sitting there thinking that this is not a big deal for you because you take that discount regardless of when the invoice is paid, you may not realize that your vendors are either billing you back for those unearned discounts or have increased their prices to adjust for your practice. It is true that the 800-pound gorilla in some markets can get away with this approach, regardless of how unfair it is, but it is not a good business practice to run roughshod over one's customers.

One accounts payable manager says that the only mortal sin in her organization is missing an early-payment discount. Her company understands the true value of this old standard. It might be worth having special handling processes that ensure prompt attention be given to those vendors that offer early-payment discounts.

THE FIRST PROBLEM

This issue relates to both those invoices that have an early-payment discount feature and those that do not. It relates to when the clock starts ticking. Usually, the customer and the vendor have a different idea of when the timing starts: The customer believes that the time starts when the invoice hits the AP department, whereas the vendor starts counting on the date on the invoice.

Companies sometimes have a difficult time processing invoices in a timely enough manner to qualify for the early-payment discount. Let's face it, 10 days isn't a lot of time when:

- Accounts payable has to receive and log in the invoice.
- A copy of the invoice must be sent to the appropriate person for approval.
- The approver has to review the invoice, approve it, and return it to accounts payable.
- The accounts payable associate has to process the invoice and schedule it for payment.
- The check has to be printed and signed in the appropriate check run, which can be as infrequent as once a week.

So companies sometimes stretch the period and take the discount a few days after the early-payment discount period really has ended, and each company's definition of what a few days is varies.

ANOTHER DIRTY SECRET

Now some reading this are probably thinking, "Why are we making such a big deal about this?" A few days can be forever, because they take the discount no matter when they eventually pay the invoice, and that is the ugly truth in many organizations. But just because they take it does not mean they get to keep it. There are companies whose sole business is collecting unearned discounts. The amount of money is not huge, but the amount of effort involved in researching these amounts when the collectors come calling should make those taking the unearned discounts think twice.

Controllers and CFOs should establish a policy regarding the taking of early-payment discounts after the discount period has ended. This is not something that the accounts payable manager should establish.

Now from a strictly financial analysis standpoint, it might seem like a good idea to take the discount no matter when the payment is made, but you need to evaluate the whole picture. This practice is not likely to endear you to your suppliers. Also, if you have relationships where you are both a buyer and seller, you need to consider how the other company is likely to react when paying your invoices. If you always take the discount on their invoices, why shouldn't they do the same on yours?

TO TAKE THE DISCOUNT OR NOT

In theory, companies should perform an analysis to determine if it is financially advantageous to pay early and take the discount. However, especially when considering a 2/10 net 30 discount, it has been years since this was anything but a cash flow consideration. When rates are higher, the analysis is an absolute requirement.

The goal—assuming that it is financially profitable to take the discount—should be to take all discounts for which the company qualifies. Many companies stretch the early-payment term for a few days and will take the discount up until, for example, the 15th day. Whatever the policy regarding taking discounts after the discount period has ended, it should be formalized and in writing.

If there is a problem getting invoices processed in 10 days, simply focus on your larger ones, where the real financial gain is. Payments, especially large ones, that involve an early-payment discount should be flagged to ensure that they receive priority handling so discounts are not lost.

DISPUTES: EFFECTS ON PAYMENTS AND RELATIONSHIPS

Inevitably, you will have a dispute with some of your vendors over invoices they send. They may have invoiced you incorrectly or there may have been a problem with the products sent, causing you to take a deduction on a payment. How these disputes are resolved and the timeliness of those resolutions will set the stage as to whether you end up with additional headaches. It will also affect your vendor relations.

Some companies refuse to pay any part of an invoice until the dispute is resolved. This ensures that cash will be applied correctly, but it can lead to additional problems. If there is a delay in payment, the supplier is likely to send a follow-up invoice in its attempt to solicit payment. As you should know by now from what has preceded this chapter, these follow-up invoices occasionally get paid. Duplicate payments are not a very efficient use of your cash. Others use any minor dispute as an excuse not to pay the invoice and to hold onto their cash a little longer. Whatever the reason, frequent delays in paying vendor invoices is likely to have a detrimental effect on your vendor relations.

TRACKING DISPUTED INVOICES

In some organizations, when there is a problem with an invoice, it effectively falls into a black hole. No one takes responsibility, and when the vendor calls looking for payment, everyone points a finger at a different department. Luckily, this happens in only a small number of companies, but it does highlight the need for a formal tracking program for all invoices, especially those with unresolved disputes.

The tracking programs can be developed simply in Excel or can be more formalized, perhaps part of the accounting system. The important feature is that once an invoice arrives at the company, everyone who needs to know can easily figure out where the invoice is in process at any given time.

ELECTRONIC INVOICING DRAMATICALLY IMPROVES INVOICE HANDLING

Electronic invoicing initiatives, also called e-invoicing or electronic billing, deliver invoices electronically usually to a centralized repository in accounts payable. The invoices can then be forwarded for the appropriate approvals. At any given point in time, there is an audit trail of exactly who got the invoice when. With the introduction of one of these programs, a lot of the game playing that used to go on disappears. No longer can someone claim to have put something in the interoffice mail two weeks ago, when they actually plan on doing it the minute they hang up the phone.

Thus, the improved tracking ends the he-said, she-said games and makes everyone behave better. Additionally, the process makes dispute resolution somewhat easier because it is often handled by e-mail. These programs also have another nifty feature that greatly enhances the resolution of disputes, as discussed following.

ONLINE DISPUTE RESOLUTION PROGRAMS

One of the neatest features in the models discussed previously is the online dispute resolution modules. These show the progress of an invoice as it works its way through the resolution steps. It also allows managers to track which invoices are in dispute and who is holding up the resolution process. Has the vendor answered the purchasing manager's query, or has the purchasing manager yet to make that query? You no longer have to guess. The answer is there in black and white for everyone to see.

INVOICE AMNESTY DAY

By now you probably realize that invoices with problems have a way of getting lost. Rather than pretending that this doesn't happen, successful department heads are introducing an "invoice amnesty day," free of finger-pointing and recriminations. Once a year, on invoice amnesty day, each staffer is asked to clean out his or her desk and submit invoices that have been sidelined for whatever reason(no questions asked). By instituting an invoice amnesty day, you will be surprised at the number of invoices that crawl out from under rocks. Such a move may also improve morale because the hidden invoices often weigh heavily on staffers' minds.

EXPLAINING DEDUCTIONS

Recognizing the fact that you will occasionally have legitimate reasons for making deductions from invoices, you will need to establish a method for communicating this to your vendors. Many organizations simply indicate the invoice number on the check stub and hope for the best. This does not help your vendors when they try to do their cash application. Now, if you are thinking that this is not your problem, you are only partially correct.

Your vendors will call your accounts payable staff demanding that they research what the deductions were for. Or, even worse, they will invoice you a second time for the amounts you deducted. In an extreme case, the vendor could end up putting you on credit hold for minor deductions. It has happened. If possible, and your accounting system allows it, include the explanation of the deductions on the remittance advice. If that cannot be done, you might want to try one of the following:

- Create a checklist that your staff could use to explain the deduction. It could be mailed with the check if you are not using self-sealing checks.

111

- Send an e-mail with the explanation to your vendor's cash application team.
- Include the information on a vendor inquiry system.

If none of these approaches will work in your department, make sure to set up a clear audit trail so you can justify your deductions. Many vendors outsource the collection of what they consider to be unauthorized deductions. If your records are not good, you could find yourself having to repay legitimate deductions.

Under no circumstances should you rely on the memory of your staff in either accounts payable or purchasing. Often the firms that work on the collection of unauthorized deductions will not get your material until 6 to 12 months after the fact. Few people will remember what happened at that point unless there was a major blowup, so, document, document, document.

SPECIAL DEALS

From time to time, the purchasing department will make special deals with customers. There are a variety of business reasons for doing this, and they frequently benefit your company greatly, but only if those special deals are actually incorporated into the purchase order and then the invoice. Unfortunately, after purchasing makes an advantageous contract, say allowing for increased payment terms, the benefit is often lost because accounts payable is never notified.

Now, you may be thinking, well, what's the big deal? The supplier will include the deal on the invoice, and certainly accounts payable will honor the more favorable terms. If that were true, nothing would be lost. However, the communication on the supplier's side often isn't much better than what's going on in your department, and the billing department over there isn't notified either. So, out goes the invoice without the special terms (or pricing or whatever). When the invoice is sent to purchasing for approval, it often gets approved because in the rush of everyday work, that special arrangement is forgotten.

There is a very simple solution to this problem. Accounts payable should be kept in the loop on these special deals. The easiest way to do this is to incorporate the terms into the purchase order. If you are thinking that this is automatically done, you are not completely correct. One best practice is to insist that purchase orders always be filled out completely.

In many organizations, this simply does not happen. Purchase orders are only partially filled out with the understanding that the standard terms and conditions will apply, and that is how special deals arranged sometimes through a lot of hard work on the part of your purchasing department are lost. It is recommended that purchase orders be completely filled out each time, regardless of whether the standard terms and conditions apply.

LATE FEES

Late fees are one of those topics that can generate lots of debate. It is also one of those issues where there is no right or wrong answer. Some vendors will automatically charge a late fee, even as one accounts payable manager explained bitterly, "if the payment is one day late." In some cases it is the vendor's way of retaliating against customers who drag their feet paying their bills. As a matter of course, some companies have a policy of never paying late fees. This is probably not unreasonable if your organization generally pays its bills on time.

Whether or not you pay late fees will depend on several factors, including:

- How much you are willing to fight against them
- Your overall payment history

113

- Your ongoing relationship with the supplier
- Whether or not you are the 800-pound gorilla in the relationship

Some accounts payable professionals (and probably some controllers and CFOs) take late fees as a personal insult and absolutely refuse to pay them. Your stance on late fees should be part of your accounts payable policy. It should be set at the CFO or controller level and be a policy that your staff will be able to follow.

For example, if most of your vendors offer 30-day terms and you generally pay in 70, it is not reasonable to adopt a "we never pay late fees" policy. However, if your organization makes every effort to pay within terms and is more than 95% successful, it might not be such an unreasonable stance to take.

PART II

Specialty Functions

While virtually every accounts payable department handles invoice processing and the ensuing payment process, that's where the similarity ends. After that, the road diverges. A number of the functions discussed in this section are handled in accounts payable, but which ones will vary from company to company. Part II looks at the problems and solutions to the difficulties in the following areas:

- Travel and Entertainment
- Unclaimed Property/Escheat
- Use of Purchasing Cards
- Independent Contractors, 1099s, and 1042s
- VAT Reclaim
- Sales and Use Tax

8

Travel and Entertainment

Without a doubt, T&E is an accounts payable function in the majority of organizations surveyed by *Accounts Payable Now & Tomorrow*. When asked where the responsibility for T&E reimbursements lay within their organization, almost 77% said it was the accounts payable department. Another 12% said their companies had a separate T&E department, while 4% indicated that it fell under the payroll umbrella. The infamous "other" category included something called accounting reviews, supply chain, and procurement. To be perfectly honest, seeing procurement fall under this heading was a surprise.

T&E POLICY

Accounts Payable Now & Tomorrow surveyed a group of its readers asking if companies had a formal written T&E policy. The news here was good. Almost 96% reported that they had a formal policy. That means that only slightly more than 4% don't have one. The news regarding updating the policy was not quite so good. While 48% reported updating it whenever there's a change, 12% updated it annually, and another 12%

said they couldn't remember the last time their policy had been updated.

The responses from the remaining 28% were all over the place. Only two of the responses were something that a best practice professional would want to hear. These included those who said they were in the process of implementing a new policy and those who had just updated it. Of course, while the fact that it was just updated is good, the fact that there is no policy for these organizations to update in the future is not.

Other responses that are not good include those that update the policy every two years or more. One party indicated that the policy was updated as needed. That could be good or bad depending on the organization's definition of "as needed." Finally, right up there with the group that can't remember when the policy was last updated are those who update it every five years.

For the record, a best practice is to update the policy any time a change is made. With the ability to publish the policy on the Internet rather than print the manual every time a change is made, this is where you should be. Updating the policy annually is also acceptable.

EQUALITY UNDER THE POLICY AND SARBANES-OXLEY

The brutal corporate reality bared its ugly teeth when *Accounts Payable Now & Tomorrow* asked if all employees were held to the policy. A full 20% of those polled indicated that not all employees are created equal in their organizations when it comes to the T&E policy. This unfortunate fact was something we suspected but were hoping to be disproved on.

If this question had been asked five years ago, the percentage of those receiving favorable treatment might have been much higher. However, since Sarbanes-Oxley, a number of companies that looked the other way when favored employees spent more than the policy might have allowed has dropped.

REIMBURSEMENT ISSUE

Reimbursement of T&E expenses opens up a quagmire that many would prefer to have left alone. As a best practice, it is recommended that all T&E reimbursements be handled electronically through the automated clearinghouse (ACH). Some companies even combine the reimbursement with the payroll payment. This seemingly innocuous approach often causes big problems with employees who demand that they receive a check instead of this electronic reimbursement.

The reason for this resistance most of the time has to do with employees hiding the reimbursement from their spouse. Whether you want to adjust your corporate policy to accommodate these requests is a matter of corporate culture and policy. However, since Sarbanes-Oxley, many of the organizations are shying away from making this accommodation.

One way to address the request for check reimbursement is to not insist that the employee receive the reimbursement in the same account as payroll. If the employee chooses to open a second account to handle this money, it is not the company's prerogative to question the reason. In fact, many direct deposit programs allow the employee to deposit money in more than one account.

ISSUES TO BE ADDRESSED IN YOUR T&E POLICY

- Administrative responsibilities of accounts payable, traveler, and approver
- Procedures for reimbursement request
- Methods of reimbursement
- Handling of nonreimbursable expenses
- Cash advances
- Approved (preferred) providers for airlines/rail and bus, hotel, and car rental

119

- Handling of lost and excess baggage
- Procedures for denied boarding compensation
- Handling of unused tickets
- Special international travel considerations, including currency exchange
- Rental car policy
- Ground transportation policy
- Use of personal automobile and reimbursement for mileage
- Lodging and receipt requirements
- Room charges
- Deposits
- Laundry
- In-room movies
- Use of telephone/fax/Internet
- Meals and incidentals, including per diem requirements
- Gratuities
- Paying for meals for others
- Meal receipts
- Travel on nonbusiness days
- Handling of miscellaneous expenses
- Policy regarding stopovers and direct flights
- Travel expense for spouse and/or guests
- Hotel rates
- Entertainment
- Nontravel business expense
- Gifts (cash and noncash)
- Who to call for information in filling out reports or with policy questions

TIMELY SUBMISSION OF T&E REIMBURSEMENT REQUESTS

Anyone involved in T&E processing for more than a few months becomes painfully aware that it is difficult to get certain employees to submit their T&E reimbursement forms on a timely basis. Let's face it: Filling out a T&E report and attaching all those annoying receipts is not a whole lot of fun. Thus, employees often delay in filling out their reimbursement requests until the last minute.

When Employees Use Their Own Credit Cards

This can cause a lot of friction in those organizations where the employee pays with his or her own credit card. Most employees in this situation need their company's reimbursement in order to pay the bill. Inevitably, several employees wait until the last minute and then raise havoc trying to get a check produced outside the normal check production cycle because their payment is due at the credit card company in a day or two.

Because this tends to happen with the same employees repeatedly, after a while the staff in accounts payable gets tired of their shenanigans. So, they refuse at some point to issue a priority check, and the employee is left to deal with his credit card issue alone or go over the accounts payable manager's head. And that is what often happens.

When Employees Use Company Credit Cards

The problem is exacerbated in those organizations where the company pays the credit card bill. In those firms, employees have little incentive to get their reports turned in on time. Or do they? *Accounts Payable Now & Tomorrow* asked accounts payable professionals as part of its T&E survey about this issue. Here are some tactics that its readers use with great success:

- Submit a report each month to the president of the company. It contains the employees' names and receipt dates.
- Have an e-mail go out under the president (or some other high-level executive)'s name asking for the late reports. Most people only have to get this note once.
- Inform senior managers and supervisors of late or missing reports.
- Do not provide any reimbursements to employees who have outstanding expense reports.
- Deactivate the credit cards until required documentation is submitted.
- Require that the employee pay all late credit card charges. Actually, the organization that uses this approach gives the employees one pass, paying the charges the first time.
- Credit card payment is not made until T&E report is received.
- Send correspondence to the employee, with escalations to increasing levels of management if the employee does not resolve the matter.
- Do not provide cash advances. If the company insists on offering them to traveling employees, restrict this privilege to those who are not late with their reports.
- If an employee receives an advance and does not submit a report within 30 days, the employee's manager is called in to explain to the division director.

You may be cringing reading this. Yes, the tactics described are harsh, but getting T&E reports submitted on time is important, and sometimes it takes a tough person to get the matter resolved.

T&E PRACTICES: SPOT-CHECKING AND CASH ADVANCES

Probably the two issues that are likely to cause the most debate when it comes to T&E are the questions of whether to give cash advances and whether to verify every detail of every expense report. We were surprised when we asked about the level of detail verification that goes on when reviewing T&E reports. When asked if they completely checked every detail of every report, 69% indicated they did. Only 31% employed the best practice of spot-checking. To be perfectly candid, we had expected the figures to be reversed. When it came to cash advances, the numbers were reversed. Only 38% of those surveyed indicated that their organizations still offer cash advances. We had expected the number to be far smaller.

T&E REIMBURSEMENT REQUEST

As automated as the accounts payable function might be in other areas, when it comes to T&E reimbursement requests, few companies are very advanced. Just under 27% report using an application service provider (ASP) model. The remainder are submitted using the following:

A form based on Excel	38%
A handwritten form	19%
Another method	16%

Some of the explanations provided by those falling into the other category included:

- It is an electronic form, although most choose to write it out
- On both handwritten and Excel forms
- Preprinted forms and receipts
- Module of accounting software
- Internal form accessible on the intranet

While there were some surprises in the data, the overall facts seem to back anecdotal observations. For whatever reason, organizations are reluctant to devote the resources to T&E that they do to other financial functions. Whether it is because of the quasi-personal nature of T&E or the fact that it is a cost center rather than a profit and loss (P&L) center is not clear. What is clear is that it appears to be one of the last bastions of unsophisticated processing in the corporate world. So, how do your practices stack up against the rest of the community?

ADVANTAGES OF ASP (ONLINE) MODELS

Many things can be done electronically that cannot be done using a manual system. They include:

- Checking for policy compliance.
- Reports to management help enforce compliance with the company's T&E policies. Once again, this removes the stigma of being the person who will not pay for unauthorized expenses from the accounts payable staff.
- Corporate charge cards are paid exactly when they are due.
- A simpler and more efficient T&E audit.
- A more efficient and therefore timely settlement to employees.
- The elimination of cash advances.

These systems allow a more efficient use of the accounts payable department's resources. This permits your accounts payable staff to move away from clerical tasks and become involved in more analytical work.

T&E FRAUD: DON'T LET YOUR EMPLOYEES PULL THE WOOL OVER YOUR EYES WITH THESE T&E TRICKS

I must be either a goody-two shoes or completely naïve because I am horrified by a book that's currently making the rounds.

Entitled *How to Pad Your Expense Report . . . and Get Away With It!* Employee X (the author) provides tips to those who want to increase their income by illegally inflating their expense reports. The staff at *Accounts Payable Now & Tomorrow* has read the slim book and made copious notes—on what companies and their accounts payable departments can do to ensure that their employees do not employ the ruses suggested in this book. What follows is a look at some of the more egregious practices advocated, a list of signs you can look for on employee T&E reports that might signal a problem, and some recommended best practices.

Danger Signs

Many of the strategies revolve around getting receipts. For example, employees booking airline trips themselves are advised to book several flights for the trip they will ultimately take. Once they have that coveted receipt for an expensive trip in hand, they can cancel that trip and book a less expensive one while submitting the receipt for the most expensive trip. Here are some things you should look for to help uncover possible fraud—and yes, fraud is exactly what these strategies are.

1. Sequential numbers on receipts, especially cash receipts. Compare several expense reports for the same employee if you suspect one.
2. If there are more than occasional handwritten charge slips, take a closer look at the entire report.
3. Too many cash receipts, especially if they look like adding machine tape, for low-cost meals.
4. Double-check the reports of employees traveling together to make sure they are not both submitting for meal reimbursement for each other.
5. Look really closely at the receipts for e-tickets. If you have the slightest doubt that the trip was taken, ask for the boarding passes. Even this will not guard against the multiple-booking strategy discussed previously, however.

Proceed carefully. Not everything that looks like a scam *is* a scam. Sometimes a handwritten receipt is legit, but a preponderance of these types of signs on one employee's reimbursement forms is generally a signal that further investigation is required. Let me point out something else: an employee who cheats regularly on his or her expense account is likely to have other problems. Many a corporate fraud has been uncovered because the individual involved got sloppy with expense reports.

Scams

In addition to the airfare scheme discussed earlier, a similar strategy can be used at hotels. Employees entitled to lower room rates, perhaps because of a convention or corporate rate, neglect to mention this when checking in. Then, after they've checked out and gotten that all-important receipt, they return to the front desk, make a fuss, and get charged the lower rate. They hold onto that first coveted invoice showing the higher rate and submit it for reimbursement.

Similar scams involve ordering food service in a hotel and then complaining and having it taken off the bill, taking a friend instead of a business client to dinner (because your boss will never check up with the client), submitting group receipts where the group members have already reimbursed you, and so on.

Drawing a Line

Dumpster diving is another practice advocated to get those sought-after receipts! How far is Employee X willing to go? Here's what he says: "Failing the above methods, there is always the old standby of going through the trash." He goes on to note that no one watches the trash, which is unfortunate because this is where most crooks get credit card numbers. You'll be happy to know he does not condone this practice. He writes, "For some strange reason, I don't see anything morally wrong with ripping off my company through expense reports, but using someone else's charge card number is not fair to fellow travelers."

There's another dishonest aspect to his practices that he never addresses either. Many of his techniques involve bullying or harassing the clerks who work in the hotels and restaurants. Telling the room service staff that the food was poor when you actually enjoyed the meal is despicable.

Some Best Practices

So, what can you do to ensure that none of your employees ask for reimbursements that they are not entitled to? Here are some suggestions:

- Have a firm policy, endorsed by upper management, that makes it clear to all employees that cheating on an expense report will result in termination. We're not talking about someone who makes a small honest mistake, but we are talking about the person who pays $178 for a plane ticket but manages to come up with a receipt for $673 and asks for reimbursement for the larger amount.

- Use a corporate T&E card. Until I read this book, I didn't think it was crucial other than for financial cost-saving reasons. Any large company with more than a few employees leaves itself open to this type of fraud if they do not use one.

- If a corporate T&E card is not used, make it clear to employees that you have the right to see the credit card bills for the account they use for business events. When in doubt, ask for the credit card bill and the one for the following month. Sometimes, the dubious refunds will not show up until the following month.

- While we do not advocate thoroughly checking every expense report, randomly select a certain percentage each month and verify every last cent on that report. Make sure your travelers know this is done.
- If your suspicions are aroused regarding any one employee, put that individual's reports on the to-be-checked-thoroughly list each month.
- Once a year, select a small number of employees who travel a lot and pull all of their reports. Look at them in total. Does anything strike you as odd? Are there sequentially numbered receipts?

What You Can Do to Stop the T&E Games Employees Sometimes Play

One of the best tools a company has to reduce the incidence of T&E fraud is insisting that all employees use a company-sponsored T&E card for all expenditures. Cash should be used only when something can't be charged. Why? The benefits of a corporate card to an organization are numerous, with one of the prime benefits being limiting the options of employees who are bent on expanding their income at the expense of their employers. These crafty employees do this by employing smoke and mirror routines on their entertainment expenditures. Here's a look at some of those tactics and the strategies you can use to counter—and hopefully thwart—them:

- Frequent requests for cash reimbursements right under the dollar amount where receipts are needed may signal a little mad money for the employee. While this will happen from time to time, check several consecutive reports to see if a pattern emerges.
- Sequential receipt numbers on handwritten receipts could indicate that the employee is producing phony receipts

from a pad purchased at a supply goods store. Again, check several consecutive reports to uncover the truth.

- Submission of the tear-off receipt from a restaurant tab. A real red danger spot is when the receipt is filled in by hand and that handwriting is the employee's. Ask to see the credit card bill showing the charge.

- Unusually high airfare for trips can signal monkey business. If the trip was planned at the last minute, the employee may have been forced to pay an outrageous airfare. If not, ask to see the employee's credit card statement and make sure he or she did not book several tickets, providing you with a receipt for a higher-priced ticket that was then cancelled.

- While e-tickets save money on one hand, on the other they provide golden opportunities for those with larceny in their hearts. If your employees use e-tickets and that is the growing trend, insist that the boarding pass be included with the T&E report. Then verify that the flight on the pass is the one on the receipt. There's still room to play here, but this process will tighten the controls.

- Request that employees turn in both the hotel invoices that detail all the charges and the credit card receipt. There are two reasons for this: As you are probably aware, the IRS has different reimbursement rates for meals. Because some employees charge meals to their rooms, the tax accountants need to break out these figures. From a fraud standpoint, this is a good idea also. Hotels frequently include an incorrect charge on their digests. Thus, if you accept the digest, periodically you may be reimbursing employees for charges they did not incur. Employees who have these amounts removed from their bill would reap the benefit.

- Does the mileage on that expense report look a little high? With the current reimbursement rate of $.485 per mile, an extra hundred miles translates into almost $50. Get on the Internet and check MapQuest, Yahoo maps, or one of the other online sites that provide directions. While the mileage won't be an exact match, it should come pretty close.

Checking T&E reports is a mixed bag. You don't want to spend so much time on it that you effectively, "spend a dollar to save a dime." However, if employees know no one is looking, a certain percentage will take advantage. The best approach is probably to spot-check 5% to 10% of all reports, along with all those over a certain dollar limit, say $1,500, and all reports of known offenders.

There is one final reason that T&E deserves your attention. Thieves rarely stop at one venue. When presented with an opportunity, they quickly step up to the plate. More than one large corporate fraud was unraveled when the crooks, who were not satisfied with what they were already raking in, tried to defraud the company by requesting reimbursement for phony expenses.

T&E FRAUD: THE GIFT CARD PROBLEM

On January 31, 2006, Tom Coughlin, a former Wal-Mart vice chairperson, pled guilty to fraud involving the theft of money, gift cards, and merchandise from the retailer that employed him. He has been accused of misusing more than $500,000 of company funds via fraudulent reimbursements. One of his tricks allegedly was to use gift cards intended for lower-ranking employees (to raise morale!) for personal expenses. His misdeeds point to yet another area that accounts payable needs to monitor.

To be honest, this is not the first time we've heard tales of high-ranking employees taking gift cards meant for rank-and-filers. Does your organization use gift cards either in the manner Wal-Mart intended or for year-end rewards? What, if any, controls and/or audits are done to ensure that the cards are used legitimately? We asked a group of accounts payable professionals for suggestions, and they came up with a number of good ones.

The Not-Pretty Solution

The first thing that accounts payable can (and probably should) do is to raise the issue. Clearly, an accounts payable manager would not be in a position to question or audit the use of gift cards by a high-ranking executive without the formal backing of the organization's management. We do not think, in light of what has gone on, that it would be unreasonable to require that executives using these cards provide a list of recipients that can be spot-checked to ensure proper use. Yes, this is definitely not a pretty solution, but the problem itself is ugly.

Some More Palatable Approaches

If you prefer a less severe approach, you might try one of the following tactics, which basically prevent the problem:

- Use e-mail to distribute gift cards to intended recipients.
- Have gift cards controlled by the company's corporate human resource representative.
- Have employees sign for receipt of their certificate/card so you have documentation that it went to the appropriate person.

Some form of acknowledgment in the form of an e-mail or interoffice memo, letter, and so forth could be used to inform the intended recipients of the reward. Included in the thank-you for your work efforts, a simple note that if they have not received the card by a certain date, to contact the sender. This alone should deter the abusers or at least cause them some concern for being found out eventually. It should not be too difficult to ensure that the number of cards issued corresponded with the messages sent to recipients.

An Alternative to Gift Cards

Recognizing the potential for abuse, more than one person suggested avoiding the cards completely. Here are two professionals' thoughts on this slant:

1. *Instead of issuing loaded gift cards to employees, certificates that can be redeemed for gift cards can be given.* This certificate would state the dollar amount of the gift card and have the signature of the employee who redeems the gift card, as well as the signature of the person giving the gift card to the employee. An employee should be responsible for loading all employee gift cards and should verify the signatures before the gift card is issued. This employee's supervisor should review the signed certificates regularly, looking for any abnormalities (e.g., the same employee receiving multiple gift cards). As a high-level control, executives can set a limit that supervisors have the ability to issue gift card certificates, and this limit can be used as a double-check of gift cards issued.

2. *Issue (redeemable at Wal-Mart only) checks for the gift card amount (e.g., $100).* Require endorsement on the reverse side of the check to include:
   - Signature
   - Printed Name
   - Employee number

Examine the cancelled checks when they come back and see if they agree with the company payroll list. While this approach would not guarantee that they were used by Wal-Mart employees, you would get some idea of how many were or were not used. At the register, verify the gift card user's name with a (required) employee ID card when they are tendered.

Don't Forget the Tax Implications

Several people pointed out that gift certificates and gift cards meant for employees are specifically listed as income to the employee, which is subject to withholding and FICA (Federal Insurance Contributions Act). All gift cards need to be included on the employee's W2 at year-end.

Unfortunately, unlike Shoeless Joe Jackson, the ball player involved in the infamous Black Sox incident, Coughlin apparently is guilty. Shoeless Joe ended up with a lifetime suspension, whereas Coughlin's penalty will likely be shorter, albeit harsher. He is expected to serve jail time in addition to paying possibly hefty fines. By following some of the suggestions discussed here, you may be able to ensure that your company does not end up with a small financial but humongous public relations nightmare as was the case discussed here.

9

Unclaimed Property/Escheat

Unclaimed property, also referred to as escheat, is an issue that often leaves controllers and CFOs (as well as hordes of other people) scratching their heads. For business purposes, it is defined as the reversion of property to the state or county, as provided by state law when the property is abandoned. There are also some inheritance ramifications, but those are not germane to this book. The concept dates back to feudal law, which is exactly where many people think it belongs. It is sometimes referred to as the process whereby states and federal agencies acquire custody of unclaimed property and abandoned assets, including uncashed checks, unpaid employment and insurance benefits, dormant bank accounts, and so on.

WHAT'S REQUIRED

Property holders must turn over unclaimed property to the states. The process, commonly referred to as *escheat*, affects every organization, whether it be for-profit or not-for-profit. That's right, not-for-profits need to comply. For most organizations reading this, the main categories of unclaimed property that they need to be concerned about include:

- Uncashed vendor checks
- Uncashed payroll checks (this often happens when an employee leaves and moves concurrently)
- Open credits

While many controllers and CFOs are aware of the requirement to escheat uncashed checks, not everyone realizes that open credits are considered unclaimed property.

Insurance companies and other financial institutions also need to escheat:

- Life insurance premiums
- Claims payments
- Dividends
- Abandoned bank accounts

LEGAL OVERSIGHT

This is not something you can ignore. The pertinent laws that govern unclaimed property requirements include:

- The Uniform Unclaimed Property Act of 1954
- A Supreme Court ruling in 1965 (Texas v. New Jersey, 380 U.S. 518)
- The Uniform Unclaimed Property Act of 1981
- The Uniform Unclaimed Property Act of 1995

TIMING OF REPORTING

Complying organizations must report to each state annually. Not all states have the same deadline—that might make the process too easy. Most states have a November 1 deadline, with March 1 being the filing date for another large group of the states. These filings must be done on time, as the states typically have a penalty for late filing in addition to the fine for nonfilers!

Some companies like to hold onto uncashed checks, eventually writing them off their books to miscellaneous income. This is a really bad idea. Because the funds related to uncashed vendor checks have to be turned over to the state and you don't get to keep the money, why not try to improve vendor relations by tracking down the vendors to whom you owe the money and give them their funds?

The recommended policy is simple: Have as few checks left outstanding as possible. This means systematically following up on all uncashed checks, not just at the end of the year. Because your company is not going to get to hold onto the funds, you may as well give them to their rightful owner.

In addition to researching uncashed checks to ensure that the funds end up in the hands of the rightful property owners, companies should establish rigid procedures for their payment processes as well as other accounts payable functions. Not only will this ensure a well-running operation, it will also minimize (if not eliminate) duplicate payments and make fraud more difficult, which will help the company minimize unnecessary escheatment.

UNCLAIMED PROPERTY: AN UNENDING PROCESS

Karen Anderson of Unclaimed Property Recovery & Reporting (UPRR) is a seasoned professional with extensive experience. She strongly recommends that the escheat process be ongoing. She suggests beginning the process in the Summer by:

Step 1: Retrieving the uncashed check list

Step 2: Selecting checks for research

Step 3: Determining which checks are eligible for due diligence letters

Step 4: Creating a compliant due diligence letter

Step 5: Timing and sending due diligence letters

Step 6: Following up and finalizing the prereport list

Step 7: Maintaining due diligence records

In an effort to make this process more efficient this year, she suggests reviewing each step to see where they can be fine-tuned. What follows are her suggestions in this area.

Retrieving Uncashed Check Information

Best practices would dictate that this step and the following one be performed well before the statutory due diligence period. Procedures should be developed to retrieve and research uncashed checks 6 to 12 months after check issuance. However, if these procedures are not in place, it is important to initiate this part of the process well before the July 1st to August 31st due-diligence-letter-mailing time frame mentioned in the fifth step.

To retrieve the uncashed check list, look to the bank reconciliation. The cumulative list of uncashed checks should be compiled from this information. This is the starting point.

Selecting Checks for Research

In some cases, checks on the uncashed check list may be there because of accounting errors and, therefore, do not actually represent payment for a debt owed. Such accounting errors are *not* unclaimed property. For this reason, it is important to research the validity of suspect uncashed checks. Generally, a materiality dollar limit will be set over which the checks can be researched to determine if they are duplicate payments, checks reissued without voiding the originals, payments for invoices for which credits were issued, and so forth.

The research may require review of the transaction source documents. For example, with regard to a duplicate payment, a professional may be able to review both transactions on the accounts payable system to see that one transaction/check has cleared and the other has not. Other accounting error research may require review of paper documentation. Once the research is completed, the list of uncashed checks is modified by deleting the accounting error reversals.

Determining Eligibility for Due Diligence

This step is the crucial one. The list of uncashed checks is narrowed to what will be reportable in the annual filing. Then it is again sorted by those that require due diligence letters and those that do not. To determine which checks are reportable, we first look at the state of the address of the check payee to identify the applicable "dormancy period."

For example, if a noninsurance corporation had an uncashed accounts payable check owed to a payee with an address in California, the dormancy period would be three years. The three years is measured from the "end date" backward. For most Fall reporting deadline states, the end date is June 30th. Therefore, for the Fall 2005 reporting deadline in California, the accounts payable checks that must be reported and remitted are those with issue dates of June 30, 2002, and prior. If the payee address in this example is in North Carolina, the dormancy period would be five years and, therefore, only checks with issue dates of June 30, 2000, and prior would be due for reporting to North Carolina by the Fall 2005 reporting deadline.

Once the "reportable" property list is compiled, the second element of this step comes into play. The list must be reviewed by check dollar amount and the state of the payee address to determine if a statutory, prereport due diligence letter is required. For example, a check to a California payee with an issue date of April 27, 2002, would be reportable to California on or before the Fall 2005 deadline. However, if the check had a value of less than $50, the prereport due diligence letter would not be required by California. This review of the "reportable" list using the state due diligence minimums will narrow the list to those checks for which due diligence is required.

At this point, it may be advisable to review the corporate vendor master list to determine if there is a new or second address for the payee of checks on your reportable list. Sometimes corporations do business with different locations of a company, and an uncashed check may be resolved by contacting a second location. Of course, materiality should be considered when setting this procedure, and a limit of $500, $1,000, or more may be used to trigger this address review procedure.

Creating a Compliant Due Diligence Letter

Basically, a due diligence letter should provide the appropriate details for the payee to determine whether the check in question represents a debt owed that has not been otherwise satisfied. However, state unclaimed property laws have particular requirements that also must be considered in creating the statutory prereport letters. For example, California requires that the notice letter include specific information, which must be in bold type or type two points larger than the rest of the notice. In any case, most states require that the content of the notice include the following:

- A statement that the property will be delivered to the state if no action is taken
- A statement that the state is the custodian and the owner does not lose his or her rights to the property after it is delivered to the state
- A date by which the owner must respond and/or a direct request for the owner to respond

- Instructions for responding (e.g., how to contact the check issuer, the methods for responding and/or receiving the property, how to effect an address update)
- Identification or description of the property

It is recommended that the payee be given at least 30 days to respond to these letters.

Timing and Sending Due Diligence Letters

The latest Uniform Disposition of Unclaimed Property Act (1995) (UDUPA 1995) states that the due diligence letter must be sent not more than 120 days nor less than 60 days prior to the reporting deadline. About 34 states have this type of requirement or a requirement with similar timing.

For corporations that have property due to a state with a Fall reporting deadline, the UDUPA 1995 due diligence timing would run from about July 1st to August 31st. Considering that a payee should be provided at least 30 days to respond, the corporation will need time to create and send a replacement check and to take other follow-up measures (e.g., recording the letters returned from the post office as undeliverable, account reconciliation), the sooner the letters can be mailed the better!

Following up and Finalizing the Prereport List

Normally, responses to due diligence letters are received within 10 to 15 days after the mailing. It is important to have a procedure for verifying that the respondent is the payee in question and for check reissuance. Once the respondent is verified as the payee, then the original check must be voided (if it hasn't been already) and so recorded. The new check must be issued and appropriately recorded as well. Of course, the reportable unclaimed property list that was compiled in the third step

141

should be modified by deleting those checks for which replacement checks have been issued and delivered.

Maintaining Due Diligence Records

Now that you have finalized the reportable property list, it would seem that the prereport preparation is complete. Unfortunately, one more step should be a part of the due diligence procedures. A copy of the due diligence letter used, along with a list of the checks and corresponding payees to which letters were sent (which was compiled in the third step), should be retained in the event that the corporation is subject to a state unclaimed property audit. State unclaimed property auditors, or the third-party unclaimed auditors that states hire, often request proof of due diligence.

After completing all of these steps, the accounts payable professional can enjoy the summer—at least until it's almost over, when it's time to separate the reportable unclaimed property list into the various state reporting formats and review the substantiation for creating the remittances that accompany the reports. Report and remittance filings occur in late October and early November. Then the due diligence process starts again—an unending process!

UNCLAIMED PROPERTY DILEMMA FOR THOSE CURRENTLY NOT IN COMPLIANCE

As most reading this are painfully aware, uncashed checks, along with certain other items, are considered unclaimed property by most states and must be turned over after a specific time period. That time period varies from state to state. (Why should anything related to accounts payable be even remotely easy or straightforward?) It's no secret that not every organization complies with the unclaimed property laws, but increas-

ingly those that are not in compliance with the escheat laws
(the legal terminology) are reconsidering that stance. Once
they decide to get in compliance, they need to do so gingerly.

Why Addressing This Issue Is Important

The states are becoming more aggressive in their search for income. They are reluctant to do so in the traditional manner of
raising taxes because this is likely to alienate voters. For most
politicians, their number-one job priority is getting reelected.

So going after companies and organizations for unreported
unclaimed property is one way to fatten their coffers without of-
fending their all-important constituency. Uncashed checks are
considered unclaimed property by the state and should be
turned over to the state. Because only a small percentage of
those funds are ever claimed by the payees, this money represents a windfall for the states—or am I being cynical? Not every
uncashed check needs to be turned over. There are some exceptions, but you need to do the research on each item and
be able to prove your stance each time you don't escheat. Otherwise, the states' auditors will cite you when they come in for
an audit.

There is another issue you should be aware of. Some auditors are actually third-party firms working on a contingency
basis earning a percentage of what they recover for the states.
Keep this in mind when we discuss getting into compliance.
Some of these auditors work for more than one state.

Getting in Compliance

From time to time, different states will offer amnesty on this
issue, but before you decide to bite the bullet and take advantage of one of these offers, read the fine print very carefully.
It is unlikely that you will be able to just start complying going

forward. Typically these offers are for amnesty of fines for past noncompliance, not for the amounts that you should have escheated. If you are not currently in compliance, there are several ways to begin complying. You could:

- Do it yourself (not recommended).
- Have a firm do it for you at no cost, as some will (really not recommended).
- Hire a firm to get you in compliance. This should cost in the neighborhood of $15,000 plus a percentage of the items the escheat experts prove not escheatable.

This issue is very sensitive. If the state gets wind that you are not in compliance, they will be in for an audit before your expert has a chance to approach them and negotiate a settlement. Don't forget, as harsh as this may sound, if you are not in compliance with unclaimed property laws, you are breaking the law. In this Sarbanes-Oxley environment, this is not an enviable position to be in.

A Word about the No-Cost Option

As noted previously, some firms will get you in compliance at no cost to you for the first year. If at first glance, this seems like an attractive option, consider the fact that I refer to this approach as the penny-wise-pound-foolish way of getting into compliance. To paraphrase Kurt Vonnegut, there's no such thing as a free lunch. These firms are compensated by the states on a contingency basis. Thus, they have no incentive to work to reduce your escheatable items, and what you pay one year sets the stage for future payments. Also, a large payment one time sets the stage for larger payments on an ongoing basis.

No matter what you think about the escheat laws, you are required to turn over unclaimed property to the states. It's the law. If your company is not currently in compliance, consider the facts and alternatives presented here and proceed with caution. For a list of companies that can help you with this requirement, go to *www.willyancey.com/unclaimed.htm#Compliance_ for_Holders*.

10

Use of Purchasing Cards

Many experts estimate that it costs anywhere from $50 to $150 to process a purchase order and issue a check. That's an extremely inefficient way to pay for a $25 widget. To many people it seemed like there had to be a better, more efficient, less expensive way, and there is: the corporate procurement card, also referred to as purchasing cards or p-cards.

These cards are typically issued by the big three credit companies: American Express, MasterCard, and Visa. Companies that have adopted use of p-cards have often radically reduced the number of invoices and checks cut in their accounts payable departments, but not without some headaches.

CONTROL FEATURES

Some organizations fear they will lose control if they give their employees credit cards. This fear is unwarranted. Most companies limit the amount that any one employee can charge in a particular time frame. Here are some ways companies control

147

p-card usage while encouraging employees to use it wherever appropriate:

- Limit the dollar amount of each transaction. Some companies set this limit as low as $50 or $100.
- Limit the dollar amount that each employee can spend in a given month. A repair person might be limited to no more than $1,000 per month, while the plant supervisor might have a limit that is 10 times that amount. Limits can be initially set low and then raised as needed.
- Use standard industrial code (SIC) blocks. For example, some companies block furriers and other luxury goods stores. The problem with this issue is that sometimes companies are in more than one line of business, yet they are limited to one SIC code. There have been instances where employees have been blocked from making legitimate purchases.
- Insist that the department manager review and sign off on all monthly statements.
- Limit the number of employees who are given the card, but don't be too restrictive; remember, you want the card to be used.

Each company should have a formal policy with regard to its p-card program. The National Association of Purchasing Card Professionals (NAPCP) suggests that the following elements be spelled out in the p-card policy given to all affected employees, including the administrative assistants of those executives who use p-cards:

- The business case so employees gain an understanding of the importance of using the process
- A definition of targeted transactions as well as those that are excluded
- Transaction and monthly spending limits

- User procedures, including initial card activation, receipt and record retention, and time frame expectations
- Preferred suppliers
- Procedures related to lost/stolen accounts
- An explanation of decline potential and appropriate procedures
- Cardholder agreement of responsibility

The policy should be updated periodically, ideally whenever a change is made or, at a minimum, once every year. These changes should be reflected in the policy and communicated to all affected employees. The policy can be published on the Internet or intranet site for easy access by all employees. New employees should be given the policy as well as an overview as part of their welcome packet.

PAYMENT TERMS

If a company aggressively pursues a p-card expansion program, it is likely to end up with a big bill. The payment terms for that bill are something that controllers and CFOs should pay close attention to. Even a few days' delay can add something to your bottom line. Conversely, paying that bill early will take a bite out of your profitability.

The NAPCP advises companies to negotiate favorable terms for the payment of the p-card bill. In most instances, payment on these cards is expected within seven days of receipt of the bill. A number of companies have succeeded in getting these terms extended to 14 and even 21 days. A company with an average bill of $1 million each month might be able to add $25,000 to its bottom line by getting the card issuer to agree to accept payment on day 21 instead of day 7, assuming it invested the money at 5%. Those borrowing at higher rates would have an even greater savings.

Although this might not seem like an excessive amount of money to many people, it's not a bad return for the few conversations it might take to get the card issuer to agree to these terms. Those just setting up a program might make the payment terms one of the negotiating points, especially if several issuers are bidding for your business.

REBATES

Companies that push large volume through their p-card programs have gone to their issuers and negotiated rebates based on volume. This is something that most issuers do not like to talk about and, in fact, many contracts forbid those who receive these rebates from discussing them publicly. How much does a company have to buy before it can negotiate a rebate? Several years ago the number was $500,000 per month, but competition may have lowered that figure.

It is unlikely that your card issuers will offer a rebate, in most cases. You will have to ask for it. Depending on the size of the company, the rebate can be an attractive feature. Some companies, in an attempt to qualify for a larger rebate, have combined their T&E cards, freight cards, and p-card into what is referred to as a one-card program.

EXPANDING YOUR PROGRAM

Once companies become comfortable with their card programs, they typically look for ways to expand the program to take advantage of the enhanced productivity as well as increase their rebates. Here are a few strategies other companies have successfully used for this purpose:

- Educating all cardholders about all the potential opportunities to use the p-card
- Expanding the number of merchants in the p-card program

- Expanding the dollar limits of those authorized to use p-cards
- Looking for new opportunities to use the card (e.g., sub-scriptions, office supplies)
- Offering cards to employees who make frequent small-dollar purchases
- Whenever an invoice comes in that could have been paid for with a p-card, sending it back to the approver, suggesting it be paid for with the p-card

ISSUES

Incomplete Data

While p-cards may be good for reducing the volume of invoices, they are not so great when it comes to the appropriate accounting. Unfortunately, most companies require a level of information for accounting purposes that is not provided by the card issuers. Even if the card issuer can provide the information, the vendor may not have the capability of inputting the necessary information. Thus, many issuers who indicate that they can provide Level 2 and Level 3 data can only do so for a portion of your suppliers. Without going into the intricate details of what this data is, know that it provides greater detail that will help with your general ledger (GL) coding.

Many companies have adapted to this issue. They either do not care or they make some gross assumptions based on the party charging the products. If a handyman at a local plant purchases a small-dollar item at a local hardware store, there's a real good chance that this is for repairs.

Employees Not Using the Card

Occasionally, an organization will have an employee or perhaps a manager who refuses to use the p-card, preferring to rely on the old-fashioned method of payment, the terribly inefficient invoice to check payment approach. This is infuriating to those who worked so hard to set the program up, especially if they are looking for productivity gains or big rebates.

Sometimes accounts payable has to play hardball in order to get these rogue employees to use the p-card. Some accounts payable departments refuse to process the invoice and issue a check for items that should have been purchased with a p-card. They simply send the invoice back to the person who made the purchase with instructions to pay the invoice using the p-card. For this approach to work, the controller and CFO have to back up the accounts payable department with this action.

Employees Using the Card for Personal Expenditures

This is the unspoken issue that many controllers and CFOs fear. What if an employee takes the card and goes on a personal shopping spree? Is it likely to happen? No. Has it ever happened? We are forced to admit that it has on very rare occasions, but this does not mean your organization shouldn't have a p-card program.

Whenever employees are issued cards, they should be given a statement to sign acknowledging that they understand that if they use the card inappropriately they can be fired immediately and without recourse. Now, here comes the harsh part of this plan. The first time you run into this kind of trouble, regardless of the reason, you will need to fire the employee and make that firing very public. Yes, this is ugly, but don't forget that using the company card for personal expenditures is stealing.

Now, we are not talking about the case where someone pulled the wrong card from their wallet and charged a $29 pair of sandals at a department store. This happens from time to time, and the employee simply repays the company. In fact, some organizations allow employees to use their corporate cards for personal expenditures as long as the company is reimbursed. Generally speaking, such a policy is not a good idea, unless there was some sort of an emergency, but that is not what we are talking about.

If you have a case where an employee goes Christmas shopping with the company card, buys his girlfriend a mink coat on the card, or some other clearly inappropriate use of the card, that is the time to take the ruthless action described earlier.

PAYMENT

The payment issue was not originally anticipated when companies began using p-cards. Many large purchasers pressured their smaller suppliers into taking the cards. Additionally, some suppliers who signed up to take the cards did not adequately think the process through and did not integrate the program into their existing processes. The result is that a small number of vendors will send an invoice for a product that has already been paid for with a p-card. Given the lack of data provided by most credit card companies, these duplicate payments are exceedingly hard to uncover unless the purchasing individual catches the error. After all, there's no way someone in accounts payable will be able to decipher the line items on a credit card bill.

There have been reports of companies receiving invoices marked "paid for by credit card" somewhere on the invoice. This statement is not necessarily in the most visible location on the invoice. These vendors cannot (or will not) alter their billing system to suppress the printing and/or mailing of invoices. Whatever the reason, it usually ends up falling on the shoulders of accounts payable to catch these *already paid* invoices. And don't rely on the purchaser, because many an invoice marked "paid for by credit card" has arrived in the accounts payable department with an authorizing signature and a note to "Please Pay."

DEPARTING EMPLOYEES

As part of your exit process, don't forget to include a provision for getting the card back. Additionally, as part of your exit strategies, whoever is monitoring the p-card program should be informed of all departing employees so they can cancel the cards. That way, even if the card is not retrieved, the employee would not be able to use it.

The information regarding reporting the departure of employees to the group responsible for the p-card program is especially important in the case of a fired employee or one who left in a dispute. These employees are more apt to use the card when they shouldn't after they are no longer in the company's employment. Unfortunately, these are the times when, in the heat of the dispute, everyone forgets about turning off the p-card.

1099s

This is an ugly one and there is no simple solution. Many companies think that because they are paying for something with a p-card they do not have to be concerned about issuing 1099s for these payments. This is simply not true. The matter gets complicated if you sometimes pay with a p-card and sometimes pay with a check. There is some hope that card issuers will be able to do this in the near future if they become Qualified Purchasing Card Agents (QPCAs), but as I write this, it has not happened.

The NAPCP recommends several practices that help get 1099s issued wherever required, including:

- **Systems Reporting.** Most p-card programs are managed through the use of internally or externally developed reporting systems. A common functionality within these systems is the flagging of 1099-MISC suppliers. The information provided by these systems will have to be com-

154

bined with other payment systems and 1099-MISCs filed. One of the challenges to be addressed using this approach is determining who notifies whom that a supplier requires the 1099-MISC flag to be turned on. The advantage of this approach is that you are not carte blanche excluding 1099-MISC suppliers, who otherwise are a good fit for the program. The disadvantage is that you must manage the communication of 1099-MISC suppliers from cardholder to program administrator.

- **Specific 1099-MISC Card.** Some end-user organizations issue a specific card that is used only for 1099-MISC supplier(s) or purposes so that the total on that/those cards is isolated. 1099-MISC reporting would be required on these purchases. The advantage of this approach is that 1099 spending is isolated. The disadvantage is the coordination required on the part of the requisitioner and cardholder.

The discussion of these problems is not meant to deter a company from using p-cards. They are an excellent tool, especially since most employees are trying to get more done with fewer staffing resources. However, those using them should be aware of the problems that may be encountered.

11

Independent Contractors, 1099s, and 1042s

January tends to be an ugly time in accounts payable. It is extra ugly in those organizations where 1099 reporting is handled in accounts payable. About two-thirds of the readers will have this process handled in accounts payable. As most readers are painfully aware, 1099s are the forms used by companies to report to the IRS income paid to independent contractors. They are typically issued each January, with a copy going to the independent contractor in question. The rules governing what must be reported, the timing of that reporting, and who can be paid on a 1099 (versus a W-2) are intricate. The IRS establishes the rules, and companies must conform to the rules or be subject to fines and penalties.

Some independent contractors would prefer that their income not be reported to the IRS and will go to great lengths to avoid providing their taxpayer identification number (TIN) to vendors.

WORKABLE TIN POLICY

Before a vendor is set up as a new vendor in the master vendor file, a W-9 should be obtained. This can be part of the welcome packet and/or vendor application, if the company uses one. It is imperative that this form be obtained before payment is made. The IRS periodically updates its forms, so companies that issue 1099s—and virtually every company must—should review the forms they use annually.

Some independent contractors will do everything possible to avoid giving your company their W-9. Some are trying to avoid paying income tax, and others are simply not that organized when it comes to paperwork. The reason is not important. You need to report properly. If you don't, you can be liable for the income tax owed by the independent contractor and fined.

Needless to say, you will have the most leverage before you pay the independent contractor. Therefore, some organizations have a No TIN, No Check policy. Technically speaking, this is illegal. If someone does work for you, you are legally obligated to pay them. That's why it is advocated that you have a No TIN, No PO policy. In other words, no one can purchase from a vendor until you have received a W-9. This avoids all sorts of hassles and minimizes the disruptions in accounts payable in January when the mad scramble to collect needed information for 1099s typically occurs.

WHAT IF THE INFORMATION PROVIDED IS WRONG?

Now you may be thinking that wily vendors will simply give you wrong information on their TIN or someone may make a typographical mistake when entering the data. The government has thought of this situation. The problem arises when the TIN provided does not match the name reported. If this occurs, the unlucky company will receive a CP2100A notice from the IRS, reporting that the TIN is missing. And, note, the IRS considers a TIN to be missing even if you provided one if it does not match the name on its records or is incorrect in any way.

You are then required to send a B-notice to the independent contractor. B-notices are not pretty. It is one of those technical quagmires that you should do everything possible to avoid.

INDEPENDENT CONTRACTOR VERSUS EMPLOYEE

So, exactly what distinguishes an independent contractor from an employee? This determination is not always an easy, and the difference is important. In *Revenue Ruling 87-41, 1987-1 CB 296*, the IRS developed 20 factors used to determine whether a worker is an independent contractor under the common law. It has been dubbed "The Twenty Question Test."

As a general rule of thumb, at least 11 of these factors must show independent contractor status under the common-law tests. If you are in doubt, contact the IRS. Here are the questions:

For the following questions, a "yes" answer means the worker is an employee.

1. Does the principal provide instructions to the worker about when, where, and how he or she is to perform the work?

2. Does the principal provide training to the worker?

3. Are the services provided by the worker integrated into the principal's business operations?

4. Must the services be rendered personally by the worker?

5. Does the principal hire, supervise, and pay assistants to the worker?

6. Is there a continuing relationship between the principal and the worker?

7. Does the principal set the work hours and schedule?

8. Does the worker devote substantially full time to the business of the principal?

9. Is the work performed on the principal's premises?

10. Is the worker required to perform the services in an order or sequence set by the principal?

11. Is the worker required to submit oral or written reports to the principal?

12. Is the worker paid by the hour, week, or month?

13. Does the principal have the right to discharge the worker at will?

14. Can the worker terminate his or her relationship with the principal any time he or she wishes without incurring liability to the principal?

15. Does the principal pay the business or traveling expenses of the worker?

For the following questions, a "yes" answer means the worker is an independent contractor.

1. Does the worker furnish significant tools, materials, and equipment?

2. Does the worker have a significant investment in facilities?

3. Can the worker realize a profit or loss as a result of his or her services?

4. Does the worker provide services for more than one firm at a time?

5. Does the worker make his or her services available to the general public?

This is not an issue to take lightly. There have been several lawsuits over this issue, and when the companies lost, the damages were in the millions, not to mention the cost of the lawsuit.

KEEPING UP TO DATE

Every year there are changes to the information reporting requirements. Make one little mistake and you could find yourself facing a fine—for every single 1099 filed. While the individual fines may not be great, they can quickly add up if you issue hundreds or thousands of 1099s.

This is why it is generally recommended that someone on your staff directly involved in the 1099/1042 information reporting attend at least one seminar a year on this topic. There are numerous ways to achieve this goal (e.g., the American Payroll Association gives many local one-day seminars each fall on this topic. IRSCompliance.org gives numerous webinars on information reporting topics throughout the year. For one low fee, your entire staff can listen in. In fact, some are given in conjunction with *Accounts Payable Now & Tomorrow*, a publication written by the author of this book. IRSCompliance.org also holds an annual conference each summer that delves into the topic in depth.).

IRS'S TIN MATCHING PROGRAM

Are you sick and tired of B-notices and dealing with names that don't match the TINs that the vendors provided? Well, you are not alone. The IRS gets one billion Information Returns, and it says that 3% of them have errors. Speaking at IRSCompliance.org's annual conference, the IRS's Pat Alfred discussed the new IRS initiative to address this problem and explained how accounts payable managers can best use this program.

Background

A TIN can be any one of the following:

- Social security number (SSN)
- Employer identification number (EIN)

- Individual taxpayer identification number (ITIN)
- Adoption taxpayer identification number (ATIN)

Given the problems engendered by mismatches, the IRS has developed a program that will allow organizations to check the match before they submit their Information Returns. The IRS wants to provide the third-party payor community with the opportunity to "perfect" W-9 data prior to filing annual reports. Not only will this help the IRS by reducing the error rate, but it will also help the payor community in that it will have fewer B-notices to deal with. Best of all, you don't have to wait until the end of the year to take advantage of the program. You can use it throughout the year as you get those W-9s, not months later when finding the vendor who provided the information is often impossible.

Eligibility to Use the Program

Accounts Payable Now & Tomorrow urges everyone who is entitled to use this program to do so. Who is authorized to participate in this great initiative? Authorized payers who have filed information returns with the IRS in one of the two prior tax years may qualify. Authorized payers are those whose EIN can be validated via the IRS's Payer Authorization File. Payers who file any one of the following documents may transmit:

- 1099 B
- 1099 INT
- 1099 DIV
- 1099 MISC
- 1099 OID
- 1099 PATR

The IRS hopes to expand the program to include other types of income. However, that will not happen soon, although they are continuing to advocate for it in the future.

Interactive TIN Matching

Up to 25 TIN/name combinations may be requested during one submission. Users can perform multiple submissions during one session. Responses to interactive requests are delivered on the screen to the user, along with an additional numeric indicator in the result field. It generally takes less than one minute to get a response. The numeric tells whether there is a match or not, and if not, what the problem is. Interpreting the results is fairly simple. Here are the results you can get, along with an explanation of what each means:

- Name/TIN combination matches the IRS records
- Missing TIN or TIN is not a nine-digit number
- TIN not currently issued
- Name/TIN combination does not match the IRS records
- Invalid request (e.g., contains alphas, special characters)
- Duplicate request

As you are probably aware, the IRS cannot provide the correct TIN if there is not a match.

Bulk TIN Matching Requests

While it is great that you can enter more than one match at a time, 25 is a drop in the bucket for some companies. That's where the bulk TIN matching program comes in handy. Before you get started, be aware that the data is returned to the sender and no one else. Bulk TIN requests are submitted to a secure mailbox via a user-configured .txt file.

Users can submit 100,000 combinations at a time. Some think that this is the maximum that can be submitted in a day. However, that is not true. There are no per-day limits on the number of files users may submit in a day.

The turnaround time, as you might expect, is not as quick as for the batches of 25. The published response time is 24 hours but in reality most often the results come back in about four hours. Each .txt file submitted will be assigned a tracking number. This enables tracking with the responses sent to the user's secure mailbox.

How Is It Working?

In the first year, 546,000 TINs were processed in the interactive program with 515,000 successful matches. Currently, the program is servicing 2,800 confirmed users. The bulk matching program had over 11 million submissions. The collective match rate for both programs is approximately 96%.

It is estimated that the interactive TIN matching program can handle just over 20 million requests each year, and the bulk matching program will be able to process 769,000 requests per year. Thus you can see that there is plenty of room to handle a lot more volume, including your business.

The eServices registration home page and product tutorials may be accessed via *www.irs.gov/taxpros/article/0,,id=109646,00. html.* You can also call the e-help desk for assistance between 8 a.m. and 7 p.m. Monday through Friday at 866-255-0654.

MAKING PAYMENTS TO FOREIGN INDIVIDUALS

Form 1042-S is used to report all nonemployee payments made to nonresident aliens and payments made to nonresident employees who claim exemption from federal income taxes due to a tax treaty. The filing deadline for 1042-Ss is March 15. Sometimes, companies don't realize that they have different reporting requirements for payments made to foreign individuals.

This issue has come under increased scrutiny after September 11, 2001. If you are affiliated with a university, you need to focus on this issue. Under the requirements of IRS Code Section 1441, any person or organization issuing certain payments to foreign individuals or entities is required to withhold tax on

164

the gross amount paid. This includes payments subject to tax under IRC 871(a) or IRC 881 (a). Generally, the rate of withholding required is 30%. However, the rate of withholding may be reduced or eliminated if a tax treaty exists with the payee's country of residence (for tax purposes), and the withholding agent (payer) obtains the required documentation from the foreign person or entity.

This documentation would consist of one of the Forms W-8 series properly completed (generally a Form W-8BEN for the beneficial owner of the income) that includes a TIN and all claims to treaty benefits on the form clearly indicated.

Failure to comply with these regulations means your organization may be responsible for the required amount of withholding. Additionally, it could be assessed penalties for failure to withhold, failure to deposit, failure to report to the IRS, and again to the recipient, not to mention interest and penalties for failures at the state levels.

In contrast to TIN certification and U.S. reporting, withholding rates on nonregistered aliens (NRAs) are not necessarily reduced or eliminated upon the receipt of a Form W-8 as compared to the Form W-9. If you are successful in obtaining the correct information on the Form W-8 or other appropriate form for NRAs, reduced treaty rates may be applied. Foreign countries have established their acceptable treaty rates with the IRS. In most cases, you will be required to withhold tax from the payment.

The requirements to certify and obtain proper documentation on a foreign person or entity are critical to properly process payments and withholding. Any area within your organization that issues payments should have up-to-date procedures in place to reduce your risks for errors and penalties related to information returns and withholding.

Additionally, the guidelines for determining if a payment issued to a foreign individual or entity is reportable can be complex. For example, when issuing a loan interest payment to a

U.S. corporation (C or S corporation), the payment is generally not reportable. However, when issuing the same type of payment to a foreign corporation, in many instances it will be reportable because the status of corporation is not the sole determining factor for reportable status.

PAYMENTS TO TERRORISTS

Clearly, controllers and CFOs want to avoid making payments to terrorists. This occasionally can happen, even in organizations having no international dealings. Refer to Chapter 3 for explicit instructions in this area.

12

VAT Reclaim and Other International Considerations

Value-added tax (VAT) is a consumer-oriented tax imposed on goods and services sold. As a taxable entity incurring VAT for business purposes, your organization may be entitled to a VAT refund in many European countries and Canada. To obtain a refund, an original invoice, together with an application form and other supporting documentation, must be submitted to the VAT authorities in the country where the expenditure was incurred. If this sounds simple, you've been deceived. It is anything but that.

Different countries have different rates, and VAT is recoverable on different items in different countries. Then there is the little issue of language. Most countries want invoices in their native language. It is a paper-intensive, heavily regulated, and deadline-ridden task. This is why it will probably come as no surprise to you to learn that most companies that reclaim VAT do so by outsourcing.

This can be a source of revenue for your organization, especially if you are not currently reclaiming VAT. While there are statutes of limitations, if you will, on how far back you can go, there is money to be had in your T&E files if your employees travel internationally and you are not currently reclaiming your VAT.

How far back can you go? Generally speaking, the limit is just one year. While this may be a bummer, it doesn't mean you shouldn't set your organization up so it can begin reclaiming in the future.

COUNTRIES ALLOWING VAT RECLAIM

If your employees travel to any of the following countries on business, you may have reclaimable VAT:

Austria	Latvia
Belgium	Liechtenstein
Canada	Lithuania
Croatia	Luxembourg
Cyprus	Malta
Czech Republic	Monaco
Denmark	The Netherlands
Estonia	Norway
Finland	Poland
France	Portugal
Germany	Slovak Republic
Greece	Slovenia
Hungary	Spain
Ireland	Sweden
Italy	Switzerland
South Korea	United Kingdom

WHAT CAN BE RECLAIMED?

The rates and items vary from country to country. However, in general, if your employees spent company money on any of the following, you may be entitled to a refund:

- Hotels
- Meals
- Car rental
- Petrol (gasoline)
- Taxis
- Public transportation
- Professional fees
- Conferences, trade shows
- Training courses
- Printing materials

The biggest payback tends to come to companies that have exhibited at conferences overseas. Depending on your line of business, you may be entitled to a large refund. Be warned, however, that it does take time to get your refunds. In an extreme case (Italy), refunds have been known to take as long as five years, although six months to a year is probably more typical.

OUTSOURCING

As mentioned earlier, most companies outsource this task. The specialized knowledge required makes this a task that few companies will want to devote human resources to. A few organizations that can help you with this task include:

- Meridian VAT Reclaim *www.meridianp2p.com*
- Tax Back International *www.taxbackinternational.com*
- The VAT Clearinghouse *www.thevatclearinghouse.com*

As well as Autovat, *www.autovat.com*, which provides software for you to do it yourself.

13

Sales and Use Tax

Sales and use tax is another of those specialty topics that sometimes falls under the accounts payable umbrella and sometimes in the tax department. Really large organizations have separate sales and use tax departments. Like unclaimed property, it is one of those areas that the states have seized upon as an income resource. A number of the states have been aggressively pursuing corporations that are not reporting correctly. With over 7,000 separate taxing entities, proper reporting can be a monumental task for any organization that operates in more than one or two different taxing entities.

DEFINITION OF SALES AND USE TAX

Sales tax is a tax on the retail sale of tangible personal property. It is important to note that it should be paid only on retail sales. It is also charged on certain services. Use tax is a little more complicated. It is charged by many (but not all) states on the "privilege of storing." In this case, storage means the purchaser's holding or controlling property brought in from out of state that is not intended for resale. Generally speaking, if goods are to be used for demonstration or display, they are not subject to use tax. The rules for what is and is not subject to use tax are very complicated and vary from state to state. It is imperative that the accounts payable professionals responsible for sales and use tax learn what their state rules are.

A few companies have no formal policies and procedures for the sales and use tax responsibility. An auditor who finds a company in noncompliance is likely to be more sympathetic to a company that has a policy in place than one that has ignored the issue. The existence of a policy indicates that the company intends to pay its sales and use taxes, even if it does not always do it correctly. The lack of a formal policy implies that the company has no plan to pay. Thus, the existence of a policy is a company's first defense against an aggressive tax collector.

Even those with a policy need to revise and update it periodically, as the laws continually change. Finally, there is one last reason to have a policy in place—the communication that goes on among states and among the different taxing authorities within one state. Many in the field believe this information is freely exchanged. Once a company is hit for backpayments and penalties, the likelihood is that other taxing authorities will come knocking at their door.

SOME TERMINOLOGY

Sales and use tax has its own terminology. Here are a few of the terms that are used, along with definitions of what they mean:

- **Absorption.** The right of the seller to "absorb" the payment of the tax on behalf of the buyer, thereby making the tax a competitive tool of price negotiation.

172

- **Consumer Levy.** The buyer has the privilege of buying and is liable for the tax with the seller serving as the trustee or agent of the state in collecting the tax.

- **Gross Receipt.** The seller has the privilege and is liable for the tax measured by the taxable sales.

- **Nexus.** A state's way of determining whether a company has a "physical presence" in the state.

- **Seller Privilege.** The seller has the privilege of selling and is liable for the tax measured by the taxable sales.

- **Separation.** The tax amount must appear as a "separate" line item on an invoice or receipt from other elements of a sales transaction.

- **Shifting.** The economic burden of paying the tax is "shifted" to the buyer.

- **Transaction.** The transaction has the privilege, with the buyer liable for the tax imposed on the transaction. In the seller's failure to add tax to the buyer's invoice, the buyer and seller remain jointly liable.

NEXUS

You should be aware that any of the following could trigger nexus:

- Ownership in the form of inventory or equipment
- Ownership of a billboard
- Maintenance by a company of a building (e.g., office, warehouse, retail store)
- Lease or rental facilities
- Presence of an affiliate (i.e., parent or subsidiary)
- Participation in a trade show

WHAT TO EXPECT IN AN AUDIT

You can expect to have your sales and use tax reporting audited. Typically, a sales and use tax audit has four steps:

Step 1: Examination of sales

Step 2: Examination of purchases

Step 3: Balancing of the general ledger sales and use tax accounts

Step 4: Review of journal voucher transactions

The examination of the purchases can be further broken down into the following three categories:

1. Purchases delivered into the taxpayer's state from out of state on which the seller did not collect tax

2. Purchases in which the taxpayer gave the seller an exemption certification where the property was not used in the manner for which the exemption was given

3. Purchases in a nonseller privilege tax state where the seller failed to collect the tax at the time of the sale

The auditors will either do detail auditing or sample auditing. Should a notice for a sales and use tax audit be received at an inconvenient time, you can ask to reschedule for a time that works better, but don't try to use this as a stalling tactic. The auditors will be back, and there's no sense antagonizing them before they even get started.

TOUGHER AUDITS

State and local auditors are becoming tougher on tax audits, warns Dr. Will Yancey, a nationally recognized sales and use tax expert. As elected leaders search for more revenue, tax audits are an important tool to extract more tax revenue and motivate businesses to comply with all applicable law. Many states are looking for more tax revenue growth from sales and use tax than from income or property tax.

Dr. Yancey notes that auditors are demanding more documentation. If you claim exemptions for resale, manufacturing exemption, agricultural use, or any other purpose, then you can expect the auditors to demand proof that you really qualified for the exemption. For inventory purchases, where you claim the resale exemption for goods and services resold to customers, auditors are now looking for material withdrawn for internal use and are assessing use tax on those withdrawals. In prior years, reasonable auditors would accept your word. Now you need specific documentation to prove you are using the purchased items for an exempt purpose.

Obtaining refunds of overpaid sales and use tax is becoming more difficult. For many years, taxpayers and their consultants conducted "reverse audits" to find tax overpayments that would offset underpayments or create tax refund claims. The states have adopted numerous rules and procedures on tax overpayments. If you overpaid sales tax to the vendor, the state may accept a refund claim only from the vendor that directly paid the sales tax to the state. Filing a refund claim often results in an audit, where the tax auditor looks for tax underpayments to offset your claims for tax overpayments.

Visibility of Sales and Use Tax

Most companies do not know the total amount of sales and use tax paid. They can look at the sales and use tax returns to see the total amount of self-assessed use tax. However, sales tax paid to vendors is usually buried in numerous general ledger accounts, Yancey notes.

Most accounts payable data-entry applications have separate fields for the sales tax and purchase amount before tax. However, most accounts payable data-entry processors use a short-cut of entering the total invoice amount without separating the tax and purchase amount. The accounts payable system can only report an accurate number for total sales tax paid to vendors when the amounts are separated during the data-entry process. If a company's accounts payable and tax professionals work together, they can develop an accurate report of total sales and use tax paid.

More than occasionally, Yancey says, managers have difficulty getting support from controllers and CFOs to improve sales and use tax compliance. Many of these executives know virtually nothing of the complexities of sales and use tax. To increase the visibility of sales and use tax inside the company, put it in the language management understands. To get more support on tax compliance and training, get the attention of senior executives by putting it in the dollars and cents language they understand. Determine the total amount of sales and use tax paid on purchases, and use this figure to start the discussion.

Broadening Tax Base

Many states are broadening the tax base to make more services and Internet-based products taxable. More states are taxing building and grounds maintenance, information services, data processing, and temporary labor. Intangible products, such as software, music, and information that could be delivered by a tangible disc or downloaded from the Internet, are becoming taxable regardless of the form of delivery. The Federal Internet Tax Freedom Act prevents most states from taxing access to the Internet but does not limit the states' ability to tax what is sold via the Internet.

States are taxing software loaded on servers and shared by multiple locations of business. To properly allocate the services among multiple locations, businesses need to allocate the purchase price among their locations based on the number of users or some other reasonable base. A new development is a multiple points of use (MPU) certificate that a business purchaser can give to a vendor. If a state allows an MPU certificate, then the seller is relieved of determining where the service is used, and the purchaser has the responsibility of determining the correct jurisdiction.

Streamlined Sales Tax

The Streamlined Sales Tax (SST) is a major collaborative project of state and local tax administrators to develop more definitions and rules that are consistent between the states. These administrators hope that if they can show simpler sales tax compliance, then the U.S. Congress will enact legislation that allows the states to compel more out-of-state sellers to collect sales tax in the states where the products are sold. The SST advocates believe the state and local governments are losing a lot of revenue from Internet-based sellers who are collecting sales tax only in their home state.

The SST has generated much interest among state and local tax administrators and corporate tax departments, but it will not do much for accounts payable departments in the next few years. The government representatives who control SST are interested primarily in sales tax collected by vendors. The business representatives following the SST are urging the states to listen to the concerns of business purchasers who have to pay sales tax to vendors or self-assess use tax.

The SST Governing Board is composed of member states that enact changes in their sales tax laws to conform to the Streamlined Sales and Use Tax Agreement (SSUTA). Some SST member states will take several years to enact the laws and regulations to fully comply with the SSUTA. Some major states that have not yet become SST Governing Board members are Arizona, California, Colorado, Florida, New York, and Texas. Thus, accounts payable professionals will still have many years where they are dealing with sellers in states that do not conform with the SSUTA.

HELP WITH YOUR SALES AND USE TAX ISSUES

If you find yourself in the uncomfortable position of having to deal with an audit, set up a best practice sales and use tax reporting program, or have other issues related to sales and use tax, there are several places you can turn. Dr. Will Yancey, CPA (*www.willyancey.com*) is a noted expert in this arena, especially if you have sampling issues. Diane Yetter of the Sales Tax Institute (*www.salestaxinstitute.com*) provides consulting services and runs training seminars in this space.

PART III

Management and Oversight Issues

Much has changed in accounts payable in the last 10 years. It is a very different function. Part of this change is attributable to the data-entry-intensive nature of the work. With the advent of the Internet, technology, and some really neat applications, this is all changing. No longer is the lion's share of the time spent simply entering invoices and checking to see that they are added correctly.

Accounts payable departments that take advantage of some of the technology already discussed plus the imaging, workflow, Interactive Voice Recognition (IVR), Interactive Web Recognition (IWR), and electronic invoicing and payments addressed in Part III are being relieved of much of the more tedious work. This has resulted in smaller, better-educated accounts payable departments, whose staff members spend more of their time addressing value-added functionality.

These value-added functions include some cash management initiatives that help their organizations drive down costs and remain competitive in the extremely cutthroat environment in which many companies now find themselves. Luckily,

179

as staffs have been upgraded in many organizations, they have become personnel capable of addressing the new concerns, primarily related to internal controls, brought up by the Sarbanes-Oxley Act.

Finally, in this part, we look at the age-old problem of fraud. This includes employee, vendor, and check fraud in all their different variations.

14

Fraud: Check, Employee, and Vendor

Fraud is a fact of life for organizations of all sizes. Those that think, "Oh, we are too small," are in for a rude awakening. Crooks have no conscience and know no boundaries. They will take from whoever they can. For the accounts payable function, fraud comes in three basic flavors (with many variations!):

1. Check fraud
2. Employee fraud
3. Vendor fraud

CHECK FRAUD

Once upon a time, when life was certainly simpler, banks routinely ate the losses associated with check fraud. But those losses grew to the point where that was no longer feasible or reasonable. In 1990, the Uniform Commercial Code (UCC) was changed, and the concepts of *ordinary care* and *comparative negligence* were introduced. These concepts are used to determine liability if there is a check fraud incident. With check fraud continuing to rocket, accounts payable needs to review what they should be doing.

How Bad Is the Problem?

The problem today is four times as large as it was in 1993—and remember that was after the banks had had enough and the UCC was changed. According to figures from The Nilson Report (a newsletter that focuses on consumer payment issues), in 2003, check fraud exceeded $20 billion per year. This is a significant increase from the $5 billion reported in 1993 and $12 billion in 1996. Looking at these numbers, it's easy to understand why banks are drawing a line in the sand and companies are taking aggressive steps to protect themselves.

Not only has the check fraud problem exploded, but the resulting changes in the UCC have also had an unintended consequence. While the goal was to reduce check fraud, the result of the change was to put corporations and their bankers on opposite sides of the table. Let's face it; if there's a loss, someone has to pay for it. And with banks no longer willing to foot the bill, the issue can get ugly.

What Does the Law Say?

First there are three parties to be considered when assessing responsibility for a check fraud loss:

1. The party that issued the check (that's your company)
2. The bank where the check was first deposited
3. The collecting bank

The idea is that each party operates in a manner that minimizes the possibility for check fraud. In articles three and four, the UCC describes the responsibilities needed under the concepts of ordinary care and comparative negligence. Generally speaking, the losses associated with a check fraud are allocated to the parties (listed previously) sharing the responsibility for the prevention of the check fraud. The allocation depends on the parties' ability to prevent the fraud. In other words, it depends on the amount of *contributory negligence* each party is assessed.

The other contributing factor is a concept called *ordinary care*. This requires that customers follow "reasonable commercial standards" for their industry or business. This seemingly innocuous statement can have significant ramifications, so don't overlook it. An organization's failure to exercise ordinary care will be considered to have substantially contributed to the fraud. Or to put it another way, the company is considered to have neglected its obligation to exercise ordinary care.

As discussed in detail in Chapter 3, positive pay is the best defense a company has against check fraud. As crooks become aware of the tools developed by industry to combat check fraud, they find ways to work around those safeguards. This has led to the development of several types of positive pay. The important component here is to know that positive pay should be used. Some will say that if positive pay is not used, the company in question is not exercising reasonable care.

DEMAND DRAFT FRAUD: THE LATEST FORM OF CHECK FRAUD

It's so mind-bogglingly easy, that it's not hard to see why crooks are so attracted to demand draft fraud. In fact, we only wonder why it hasn't become more popular with those who would rather spend their time filching your money than earning it honestly. What follows is an in-depth look at demand draft fraud, how it is executed, what your obligations are under the law, and what you can do to protect your company.

Background

If you're scratching your head wondering what demand drafts are, you are not alone. This little-known payment device was designed to accommodate legitimate telemarketers who receive authorization from consumers to take money out of the consumer's checking account. This payment alternative is very similar to writing a check, except that it requires no signature.

In place of the authorized signature on the check, the words "signature not required, your depositor has authorized this payment to payee" or similar wording is used. Because the check processing areas at banks are completely automated, the signature line is virtually never checked. In the telemarketer example, this is a creative payment approach that enables the transaction to proceed smoothly. Demand drafts are also sometimes referred to as remotely created checks.

You can see there is potential for check fraud in this arrangement, but then any time a check is used for payment, there is also the possibility for abuse. Once the thief has the account number and the name of the account owner, check fraud is merely a matter of conscience, opportunity, and a few dollars for technology.

A company called Qchex.com dramatically lowers the bar for entry. No longer is it necessary to have those few dollars for technology. It's not even necessary to know the name of the account holder, only the account number and the routing code.

What Is Qchex.com?

It advertises itself as "an interactive online platform that provides finance management and payment automation services to small businesses, consumers and institutions." It compares itself to Quicken/QuickBooks, MS Money, or VersaCheck, while claiming to be more comprehensive in its scope and available online globally. Checks can even be delivered by e-mail and printed by the recipient.

Accounts can be opened by individuals, merchants who want to accept checks, and businesses and institutions who want to send checks to suppliers or receive payments from customers. Unfortunately, Qchex does not verify that the person issuing the check is the actual account holder. It "emphasizes that Qchex does not invade the privacy of the business or interfere with financial transactions of its users. As an analogy, we would not expect the U.S. post office to open every letter or parcel we send and censor content." It claims it stops fraud because it encourages everyone to "register" their accounts. If you get there first and register all your account numbers, no crook can try and claim one of your numbers.

As you might imagine, demand drafts have become increasingly popular with those who find check fraud an appropriate way to support themselves. With Qchex, their task has become even easier, and the results have been ugly. How bad is the problem? One institution involved indicates that over 70% of the demand drafts it encounters are fraudulent. And *that* is a serious problem.

The problem has gotten so out of hand that the Federal Reserve is considering a proposal to set a new standard that would put the liability for fraudulent drafts on the bank that cashes the demand draft in the first place. This would place the responsibility to authenticate the draft with that institution. It will be interesting to see how the banks react to this proposal. It would also add some additional protections. The paying bank would have 60 days to return bad checks and consumers' rights would be spelled out. A few opponents have even suggested banning demand drafts, but that does not seem to be a likely outcome.

What You Can Do

Companies can do several things to protect themselves against this type of fraud:

- Be careful with your bank account numbers. Do not give them out unless there is a good reason.
- Keep bank account information in a secure location and only give it to employees who need the data. Do not keep a list of all bank accounts lying on your desk where anyone who comes by can see it.
- Use positive pay.
- Reconcile your bank statements in a very timely manner.
- Consider increasing the use of purchase cards (p-cards) and automated clearinghouse (ACH) payments.
- Don't automatically deposit every small-dollar check that comes in the door. Some crooks send small-dollar checks as a means of getting the company's bank account information. It shows up on the back of deposited checks.
- Reconcile all incoming checks and deposit only those from companies with whom you have an ongoing business relationship.
- Use different bank accounts for deposit activity and payments. Then, if the crook does get bank information from the back of a small-dollar check, he won't be able to use it and you'll have the last laugh. He'll have given your firm a few dollars and gotten useless information for it in return.

EMPLOYEE FRAUD

Unfortunately, you have to be careful with your employees. They are often overlooked in the bigger picture. What's worse is that when employee fraud is uncovered, companies are often so embarrassed by their own lapses that allowed the fraud to occur in the first place that they often fail to prosecute. Often the employee is let go and repayment is demanded. So, what do you think the employee does? He (employee fraud is slightly more likely to be committed by a male) goes to another organization and repeats the crime, rarely, by the way, completely repaying his former company for the stolen funds. Even more frustrating is the fact that even if the company chooses to file charges, the chance of it going to trial are very low, and the odds of a conviction are small.

Lastly, you should be aware that employee fraud is typically committed by long-term trusted employees, not newly hired suspect individuals. This is why most banks require employees to take two consecutive weeks of vacation each year. Now, if your company only gives two weeks' vacation, enforcing this policy is probably not possible. However, it does highlight why segregation of duties is so important.

SEGREGATION OF DUTIES

Checks and balances are extremely important in accounts payable. After all, your accounts payable staff has access to your organization's money. Most experts recommend that tasks be assigned so that one individual would not have access to several functions that would effectively allow that person to steal without another's knowledge. True, this can be overcome if there is collusion, but that is harder to achieve.

Some functions that should be segregated in accounts payable are:

- The person responsible for bank reconciliation should not:
  - Handle unclaimed property reporting
  - Be a signer on a bank account
- The person who is a check signer should not:
  - Authorize an invoice for payment on an account that he or she is also a signer
  - Have ready access to the check stock

- A person who is responsible for the check stock should not:
  - Be an authorized signer
  - Handle the bank reconciliations
- The person who is responsible for the master vendor file should not:
  - Be an authorized signer
  - Be able to approve invoices for payment
  - Handle unclaimed property
- The person responsible for unclaimed property should not:
  - Have responsibility for bank reconciliation
  - Have access to the master vendor file

As you review your own operations, you will probably be able to come up with additions to this list.

DESKTOP COMPUTERS: HANDLE WITH CARE*

Any company wishing to protect itself will typically ensure the correctness of its source data, internal operations, and output by testing its mainframe, server, Web applications, and upgrades for evidence of external and internal controls before going live with the applications. Similarly, the controls surrounding these applications, as well as general accounts payable policies and procedures, have come under closer scrutiny in light of Sarbanes-Oxley. But what about your desktop applications? What testing and reviews take place around those functions?

We're talking about those small local processes or workarounds maintained on a desktop such as home-grown custom

---

*The information on desktop computers is based on extensive input from Bob Lovallo, president of Pinpoint Profit Recovery, a duplicate payment audit firm.

applications, spreadsheets, and databases that crop up in many organizations where the output is used to determine a company disbursement.

Example

Some firms track their escheatable items on an Excel spreadsheet. When bank accounts are closed, as they inevitably are, outstanding checks have to be dealt with. Some organizations leave the accounts open until all outstanding checks clear. Typically, a few checks are never cashed. After proper research they may be deemed escheatable. In this case, the appropriate information was entered onto an Excel spreadsheet, the accounting entries made, and at the appropriate time the items were turned over to the state. So, what's the problem, you ask?

At the firm in question, someone was changing the entries on the Excel spreadsheets. The change did not cost the company a red cent, so its financial records were never affected. What some fraudster was doing was changing the name of the company to whom the funds were owed to the name of an individual. If this "adjustment" had not been detected, the individual would have been able to collect the funds free and clear from the state, and no one would have been the wiser.

Could this happen at your company? This is just one example of a transaction that would typically fly under the radar in many organizations. Clearly, a process to ensure the integrity and accuracy of the data in your desktop applications should be a high priority.

Overview

Normally, disbursement data is entered in, and resides on, an online accounts payable application where formal and applicable disbursement controls are in place. However, when the accounts payable data source from a desktop application does not contain essential business controls and documented procedures, then there is a real exposure to both fraud and inaccurate payments. Some of the issues every controller and CFO needs to consider are:

- Are your critical disbursement sensitive data and files residing on desktop computers secure enough to prevent the introduction of improper data or revision of proper data?
- Are the data and files protected to prevent unauthorized access, which can lead to and result in a fraud?
- Is there an audit trail and controls in place that support the integrity of source data and file additions, changes, deletions, and output?
- Do you have an inventory list of such sensitive disbursement files and applications?
- If you do have an inventory, have you performed an ongoing security check and audit for data integrity by determining the correctness of the source data?
- Do your desktop procedures include a flowchart indicating what control points are in place to ensure that control and auditability is evident and maintained?
- Do your procedures also address and maintain appropriate segregation of duties?
- Have you tested a portion of original source documents, formulas, report computations, and controls to the desktop application's output?

It is important that information at every step of the process has appropriate controls in place. You will need to verify the input, the calculations, and the output.

Recommendation

To get the fraud-prevention ball rolling on your desktop applications, a formal audit review process should take place on a periodic basis. Its purpose is to verify that desktop applications have met control assessment criteria by inspection and certifies the application output provides accurate data to accounts payable. This will better protect the company against fraud.

The inspection or review should contain a formal rating for the controls and auditability found in the application, so management can be made aware of any control problems and their severity. The bottom line is that a structured application review and postreview audit report process needs to be adopted. It should assess the adequacies of desktop application control points and audit trails to confirm that the application is doing what it is supposed to do.

If the reviewers identify specific control problems, they should recommend what corrective actions the application owner must take to eliminate the application control weaknesses and ensure those steps are taken. Often, the authority to implement this type of review lies outside the accounts payable department. Only the controller or CFO or an authorized designee with that high level of authority can add and enforce these additional controls to desktop applications. If management is willing to take action, they can better protect themselves and the company against fraud and erroneous payments; in most companies, such small desktop applications receive little or no financial management visibility.

Preventing Desktop Fraud in Your Organization

Take the following steps to ensure your desktop applications are not and will not be a breeding ground for fraud:

Step 1: Take a company-wide inventory of all desktop applications where the application output data is the source for any company disbursement.

Step 2: Develop a schedule to formally review and certify that proper procedures, controls, and audit trails are evident in each application.

191

Step 3: Assign a level of management responsible as a requestor for a particular disbursement as the OWNER of the application (every application must have an owner). For example, the tax department sends accounts payable a list of payees and amounts for state sales tax payments that originated from a desktop application; therefore, the sales tax manager would be that application's owner.

Step 4: Every such desktop application must have written desk procedures.

Step 5: The controller (or designee) must determine what basic controls all desktop applications must contain to ensure the accuracy of the application's input, output, calculations, and operations. For example, should all such applications be password protected, or can payee names be overridden and revised? (Most of the "audit for" criteria may already be in place as part of procedures and control reviews used to implement mainframe, server, or Internet-hosted applications.) The controller's "audit for" criteria or control assessment guidelines will be used to determine if desktop applications possess the necessary controls and enable the application to be audited properly. The guidelines also verify that the desktop application is providing accounts payable accurate disbursement amounts and payees. Adopting formal control-assessment guidelines will ensure that all desktop applications audits are consistent with the controller's audit criteria, are thorough, and are used as a common list for all internal audit teams when auditing any desktop application. Furthermore, deficiencies can be readily identified and communicated to the application owner as to what and where corrective actions are required.

Step 6: In order to assess the severity of the control and audit-trail deficiencies, the findings should be measured by the review team against control-assessment guidelines.

Pick a rating scale, perhaps 1 to 5, with 5 being the worst, or rankings like High Satisfactory—No Reply, Satisfactory, Low Satisfactory, and Unsatisfactory, and so forth.

Step 7: The controller or designee (possibly internal audit) should name an independent review team consisting of a financial person and an IT specialist (e.g., person knowledgeable with desktop applications, such as, Excel, Access) to conduct the review of the designated applications to confirm and test for payment accuracy.

Step 8: The review team should assess the application's control posture based on the control-assessment guidelines developed in Step 5.

Step 9: The application owner must make an immediate fix, possibly manual intervention, if the review team discovers evidence of inaccurate payments.

Step 10: Subsequent to the completion of the application review, the review team must notify management by issuing a formal report with a control posture rating (Step 6) to the controller or designee and to the application owner, documenting control weaknesses found along with recommendations the application owner must take to eliminate the deficiencies.

Step 11: The application owner must provide the controller or designee with a written response within 30 days that addresses what actions were taken or will be taken to remedy the control deficiencies, along with completion dates.

Step 12: Don't take any chances. Once the application owner states that all control or processing deficiencies noted in the review teams report (Step 10) were corrected, the review team must reinspect the application and certify in writing to the controller that the application meets the control-assessment guidelines adopted in Step 5.

Step 13: Once the application is certified, future changes in the desktop application cannot be made by the owner without a formal independent review of a preimplementation test of the application change to obtain an updated certification.

Step 14: Accounts payable must maintain and keep current the list of desktop applications, denoting which applications have been certified.

Step 15: Understanding that there is a risk of inaccurate payments and fraud for any legacy or proposed desktop application that has not been certified by an independent review team, the controller or designee and accounts payable must understand the magnitude of the risk and the exposure it presents. Assessing the application's control posture, its payment volumes, and its dollar value, the application owner should evaluate the nature of the risk and communicate the risk assessment to management. Then the risk assessment must be accepted by the CFO, controller, or their designee.

Step 16: All new desktop applications should be certified prior to their implementation.

Step 17: The desktop application list should be given to internal audit. The list should be subject to periodic audits.

Concluding Thoughts

In order to implement every step in the plan I recommend would be an expensive endeavor—one that not every company would be willing to take on. Each organization has to weigh its risk tolerance against the potential exposure and loss and then come to its own decision. Implementing even just a few of the steps will provide some level of control. In the long term, if desktop applications are left without scrutiny, my experience says that a lot of damage can be done by disbursing incorrect amounts and/or to incorrect payees, not to mention being a *breeding ground for fraud.*

PHONY VENDORS

Unfortunately, many fraudsters would rather earn their living by trying to dupe legitimate organizations like yours out of a few dollars than earn an honest day's living. These crooks will invoice your firm for goods and services that were never ordered and often never received. They count on overworked and understaffed accounts payable departments and department heads to pay these invoices, and unfortunately, that's exactly what happens in enough cases to keep these crooks thriving.

The most typical scams involve invoices for:

- Toner cartridge and/or paper for copier machines
- Yellow pages ads never placed
- Help wanted ads never placed

Because these invoices are typically for a low dollar amount, they are often not researched and just paid in the course of the day's work. This just encourages another phony invoice. So what can you do? Clearly, it is important that those approving invoices actually look at what they are signing and take the time to review the invoices' legitimacy. Additionally, many organizations have a process for new vendor verification. This process typically puts an end to the scams—at least in the organizations that use them.

UPFRONT VENDOR VERIFICATION

Establishing proper controls when adding a new vendor or updating the master vendor file will reduce your exposure to fraud. This issue is overlooked in numerous organizations. To gain increased efficiencies and productivity, accounts payable and procurement applications rely on the use of Internet and intranet technologies to update the master vendor. Use of these technologies actually presents an opportunity for accounts payable to improve internal controls and at the same time may present internal control challenges when updating the master vendor file.

Control Challenge in Real Life

Despite significant investment in internal corporate controls in the wake of the Sarbanes-Oxley Act, according to a recent global study by PricewaterhouseCoopers and the Martin Luther University in Germany, corporate fraud increased 22% over the last two years. The study also noted that most corporate fraud was detected by accidental means. Therefore, implementing preemptive internal control enhancements will only help in your attempt to minimize your exposure to fraud, especially when the integrity of the master vendor file is to be maintained.

During a recent client recovery audit Bob Lovallo was involved in, the accounts payable headcount was reduced when the company installed an accounts payable–linked front-end intranet application. The new process allowed and authorized non–accounts payable employees to enter invoice and account code data as well as access the master vendor file to identify the vendor number, and so forth. The data was edited for completeness and for valid account coding before it reached the accounts payable application and accounts payable processor.

When the invoice and the approved input document were received in accounts payable, the processor would perform his or her normal processing and approval routines. What caught Lovallo's attention was that the process now allowed employees who performed the front-end invoice processing to establish a new vendor in the master vendor file. Although the new vendor had to be approved by an independent party, he felt the new process opened accounts payable up to potential employee mischief and fraudsters. Although accounts payable increased its vigilance over the new process, some additional actions using the Internet to guard against potential fraud involving the master vendor file needed to be taken.

What follows is a look at some recommendations Lovallo suggests controllers and CFOs use to limit the potential for vendor/employee fraud related to establishing a vendor.

Who Is Confirmed   First, verify that new vendors with significant first-time payments are legit. Also, check payments to vendors who provide only a P.O. box as a remit to or address. In the past, when I worked at IBM, we used Dun & Bradstreet (D&B) and other manual means, such as the yellow pages, phone contact, and so forth, to confirm authenticity. Today it is much easier to perform this check on almost every new vendor using the Internet to check yellow pages, run Google searches, and access sites such as D&B and Hoover's.

Why Front-End Verification Is Important   This is important because there are several front-end accounts payable systems. For example, the employee prints out the cover sheet, obtains management approval (signatures) on the cover sheet, attaches the invoice to the cover sheet, and forwards the packet to accounts payable for payment. In such front-end systems where every field must be completed by the invoice submitter, mischief can occur.

Therefore, Lovallo believes it is critical to have vendor verification to prevent fraud when new vendors can be added by employees or even other company-assigned employees. You may want to address this issue by adding another separate vendor verification control point.

New Vendor Verification Guidelines Someone who is not directly involved in setting up the vendor entry should perform a double-check. Any vendor who submits a P.O. box for an address and no telephone number deserves a little additional scrutiny. Many organizations do not have the staff to verify every new vendor. Thus, they are forced to verify only a portion of the new vendors. Use the checklist on the following page as a guideline for your staff if they cannot verify every vendor. But, don't decide not to verify at all.

Should you take the step of not verifying at all, your staff will become aware of this fact—and that can get you into trouble. Remember, fraud is committed by long term trusted employees, especially those who know where the weaknesses are in your processes. And, not verifying new vendors is definitely a weakness that they will be able to exploit very easily. So, don't give them the chance.

When verifying a new vendor, one of the first places to check is the yellow pages. Not every legitimate vendor advertises there. In fact, depending on your business, you will find that many don't, so be sure to use the online resources discussed earlier. During your cross-checking, keep a record of where you found the verification information. Each company will need to select the criteria that it wants to check, the items that it thinks will protect it the best.

One Last Technique Even if you don't actually verify vendors in accounts payable, you can tell people that you do. Put a little blurb on your material saying that "New vendors set up outside accounts payable will be verified by accounts payable." This warning will help scare off petty theft. The unscrupulous will have to be a little more creative if they want to defraud your organization.

Similarly, you can create a long list of items verified—even if you don't check everything. This is one place where it is perfectly acceptable for accounts payable to be less than 100%

198

honest. With limited staff, a little creative license is sometimes called for. This helps protect against collusion within the process, since ideally the person checking in accounts payable is not the person who sets up the master vendor list. If your organization does not do this, your organization is being exposed to fraud because vendor theft is among the easiest types of fraud to commit.

Vendor Verification Criteria

Many organizations don't have the necessary resources to verify all new vendors; in those cases, verify the following:

- Vendors whose invoices do not have invoice numbers
- Vendors with P.O. box addresses
- Any new vendor over a certain dollar amount
- Vendors who submit handtyped invoices
- Any new invoice that looks odd
- A certain percentage of all new vendors

15

New Technology Initiatives

If there's one function in the corporate environs that is being radically affected by technology, it is accounts payable. All I can say is, "it's about time!" We've gone from accounts payable being the last kids on the block to get new computers (in fact, 10 years ago, they often got the castoffs from other departments) to being pushed toward the top of the list. Much of this has to do with the innovations in the payment world that now require better computers, as well as highly skilled people to run them and make the most of them. In this section we'll discuss three interrelated initiatives:

1. Imaging and workflow
2. IWR and IVR
3. Electronic payments and invoicing

They all have to do with improving the efficiency of the accounts payable operation, primarily by:

- Getting the paper out of the process
- Limiting the number of exception items that get lost in the process

- Reducing the number of phone calls from vendors looking for money or information
- Eliminating some of the game playing that goes on between accounts payable and everyone else in the company (primarily accounts payable)

Okay, the last item is not really a goal for most organizations, but it is a welcome outcome. With the audit trail produced by the processes we are about to discuss, it is no longer possible to claim to have done something two weeks ago when you actually sent something this morning.

IMAGING AND WORKFLOW

Imaging can be as simple as a small scanner such as the ones that many consumers have at home hooked up to their personal computers (although this is not really recommended for robust business applications) or a more complex process. Imaging consists of:

- Capture and index
- Delivery
- Storage (both online and archived)
- Retrieval

The most critical step in the procedure is the capture and indexing phase, since the other steps depend on it. Most companies that use imaging do so for a variety of reasons.

Once the information has been imaged, it can be forwarded to the appropriate parties using workflow. The most prominent marriage of imaging and workflow in accounts payable occurs when it is used with invoices, first imaging them and then forwarding those images to the appropriate parties for approvals. Workflow can be programmed to include escalating approvals, thus eliminating the problems associated with recalcitrant approvers.

ELECTRONIC INVOICING

Electronic invoicing, also referred to as e-invoicing or Web invoicing, is the electronic delivery of invoices, mostly over the Internet, to the accounts payable department. No paper invoice is received. The accounts payable department forwards the invoice, via e-mail, to the person who needs to approve it. The information is then available, without further keying, to be housed on a network for data retrieval purposes. This process integrates nicely with imaging and workflow.

Companies interested in pursuing the e-invoicing route will base their decision on their:

- Existing internal processes
- Budget
- Corporate culture
- Willingness to mandate changes both internally and externally

Most payment professionals don't have to be convinced of the benefits of electronic invoicing. Many embraced the concept with open arms, even if they couldn't convince their organizations to adopt it initially. Just being able to accept invoices electronically and forward them to purchasing for approval seemed like a miracle in those beginning days, but a lot has happened since then. The products have evolved, and companies can now expect a lot more robust products with increased capabilities.

Background

The term *e-invoicing* encompasses a wide range of applications. Technically speaking, the soup-to-nuts concept is referred to as electronic invoice presentment and payment (EIPP). It refers to the concept of an invoice being sent electronically, received electronically, and the ultimate payment being made electronically, most frequently through the automated clearinghouse (ACH).

In an ideal world, the entire process would be handled electronically, but some companies are equipped to handle only one end of the process, either the invoicing or the payment side, in this manner. It is generally recommended that companies move whatever portions of their accounts payable processes to this functionality as they can.

Thus, if a supplier can only accept payments electronically but cannot submit invoices electronically, pay them electronically and hope that some day soon they will be able to provide you with an electronic invoice. Some companies get around this shortfall by imaging all paper invoices received and then moving them electronically within their organizations. Similarly, if you can accept invoices electronically but are not able to initiate payments electronically, join the game that way and work on the second side of the equation.

The Basics

E-invoicing encompasses many different formats and approaches. At its simplest, e-mailing an attached Word, Excel, or PDF document should be considered electronic invoicing, because the document has arrived electronically at the customer. Similarly, a company that pays its employees using direct deposit is making electronic payments. In each of the examples mentioned, the companies involved are participating in EIPP, albeit in a minor way.

A new report from Forrester Research delineates some of the basic attributes, or what it calls core functions, of EIPP. The report called "The Forrester Wave™: Accounts Payable EIPP" says with regard to core functions that:

> Invoices can be automatically checked for required data and against purchase order terms. Self-service is embedded in the

application, enabling buyers and sellers to come to terms with one another through online dispute management, automatic reconciliation of invoices to purchase orders, receipts, and realtime status reporting. Multicountry support has become a standard, although the countries supported vary by vendor.

Additional Functionality

Although in the beginning years, the emphasis may have been more on the billing side, the payment side has gotten some attention in recent years. Look at how Forrester describes some of the expanded functions:

> Functions like automated routing developed in the past few years as EIPP vendors crossed the threshold from addressing minimum invoice-approval requirements to embracing straight-through processing (STP). Payers can automatically route and approve invoices and match invoice data to multiple document types to better manage their spending. They can also integrate with third-party financiers for more automated trade financing capabilities. Suppliers can now automatically reconcile invoice payments to their accounts receivable.

While on the face of it, the ability of the supplier to automatically reconcile invoice payments to their accounts receivable may not seem like an advantage to accounts payable, but it is. Here's why: The faster a supplier is able to apply its cash, the less likely it is to call an accounts payable department looking for its money, and anything that translates into fewer calls into the accounts payable department is a good thing for departmental productivity. It also frees processors' time to work on more value-added functions and removes some of the stress. The ability to better manage spending also helps elevate the accounts payable function.

FORWARD-THINKING FUNCTIONALITY

Finally, for those organizations looking to completely integrate their procure-to-pay cycle, Forrester identified strategic functionality across the supply chain. The report says that:

> Leading vendors include strategic functions such as procurement, electronic payments, cash management, and accounts receivable EIPP. In the future, we expect customers with accounts receivable EIPP to expand their vendor relationships to include accounts receivable EIPP solutions as well. Likewise, we expect customers who start with accounts receivable EIPP to expand their scope to purchasing and cash management.

Clearly, this integrated approach to the function will lead to further productivity enhancements and cost savings.

What is clearly apparent as terms like e-invoicing and EIPP become part of the everyday vernacular is that electronic invoicing is fast becoming the norm, not only in the realm of leading-edge companies but everywhere. It is no longer a sophisticated concept for the bleeding-edge elite but something that every company must integrate into its daily processes. The only question now is not when, but rather how much of this new technology your company will use.

ELECTRONIC PAYMENTS

If you are looking to reduce costs in your accounts payable operations, then you know that one of your costly processes is that of issuing a check. It is also an area where there is a certain amount of risk, because check fraud continues to be a problem for the corporate world. Thus, companies in growing numbers are moving toward paying their suppliers electronically, much the way they do their employees. The direct deposit concept is finding wide acceptance in the corporate arena. Interestingly, this is at companies of all sizes.

As discussed in Chapter 16, companies are renegotiating their payment terms with partners to pay them electronically. It's a win-win situation for both parties involved.

B2B ACH PAYMENT AWARENESS AND USAGE IN THE MIDDLE MARKET

It seems everyone is paying their bills electronically today, doesn't it? But are the corporations they work for as sophisticated as their staff when it comes to bill paying?

Recognizing that most of the studies to date have analyzed the behavior of large companies, the North American Clearing House Association (NACHA), the electronic payments association, decided to investigate the other end of the market. It commissioned an independent market research firm to evaluate awareness and usage of ACH services among small and midsize businesses. It should be noted that even at the very largest companies, use of business-to-business (B2B) ACH payment mechanisms is not universal. What follows is a look at the results of the study, including an analysis of the barriers to usage and what accounts payable professionals can do to overcome those obstacles.

The Survey

Although the survey analyzed activity for direct deposit and payment card activity as well as B2B ACH payments, this section will only focus on the latter. The whole report can be accessed from the NACHA Web site (*www.nacha.org*). The survey focused on two types of companies:

- Small companies—those with 2 to 49 employees
- Midsize companies—those with 50 to 499 employees

The results were reported for each company type and then for the group in its entirety.

The Finding

When it came to B2B electronic payment activity, the only people surveyed were those with at least some responsibility for accounts payable. Here's what they found:

- Four out of five respondents from midsize businesses and two-thirds of those from small businesses are aware that they can use the ACH for payments to vendors or other trading partners.
- Only one in four midsize businesses and one in seven small businesses, however, are currently using B2B ACH payment. Payment to trading partners for products or services is the most common use, although only one in nine respondents make payments in this way. Use for other types of payments, including utility, rent/mortgage, or any other purpose is less than 5%.
- Among users of ACH for B2B electronic payments, satisfaction is quite high, with nearly 9 out of 10 extremely or very satisfied.

Barriers to Usage

Why, given the high level of awareness of ACH, is usage not higher? In fact, only one in six respondents not currently using B2B electronic payments expects to start usage in the next year. NACHA wondered too. Here are their respondents' reasons, along with the percentage:

- Do not know if vendors/trading partners accept ACH payments (28%)
- Believe ACH is designed for larger companies (25%)
- Concerned errors would be hard to correct (23%)
- Not aware that bank offers it (23%)
- Too expensive (22%)

- Concerned about errors (17%)
- Too complicated (14%)
- Don't have time to learn how to handle (14%)
- Concerned about safety and security (14%)

It will probably come as no surprise to learn that when awareness and usage are combined, midsize businesses are almost twice as likely as small businesses to use B2B ACH payments (25% vs. 14%).

Satisfaction Ratings

The old "Try it you'll like it" adage certainly applies to ACH. Nearly 9 out of 10 users of B2B ACH payments are either extremely (34%) or very (53%) satisfied with their experience. This is a good prognosis for future growth. NACHA's point that the high level of satisfaction should be used in marketing efforts to attract more small and midsize businesses to this service is a good one. Accounts payable professionals trying to get a program up or expanding their existing program are advised to broadcast this fact when touting their plans.

On average, current users have about three years of experience with B2B ACH payments. Thus, concludes NACHA, it is reasonable to expect that usage will continue to expand over the next few years. In fact, 15% report that they plan to use ACH within the next year.

Overcoming the Barriers

What can professionals do when they want to expand usage or perhaps even launch a program in the light of resistance? Well, money always talks. When asked if a money-saving incentive from a vendor or trading partner would accelerate plans for usage of ACH for electronic payments, a whopping 64% responded affirmatively. Typically, in the accounts payable world, this could mean slightly extended payment terms or an extension of the early-payment discount period.

Other tactics that could be tried include:

- Educating suppliers about the benefits to the suppliers' operations
- Showing management a bottom-line savings attributable to an ACH payment program
- Including a flyer with all checks mailed offering to pay electronically

What the NACHA study demonstrates is that ACH payments are an extremely viable payment alternative and one that is likely to grow rapidly. Accounts payable professionals can add value to their organizations (and their reputations) by making sure their firms are on the leading edge when it comes to paying through ACH.

UPICs

Do your vendors refuse to give you their bank account numbers so you can pay them electronically? Do they say they are concerned about their banking information being used fraudulently? Well, you are not alone. Given the general concern about sharing banking information, it became apparent a while back that a universal intermediary was needed. This was the genesis of the Universal Payment Identification Code (UPIC).

Background

A UPIC is a banking address used to receive electronic credit payments. It acts exactly like a bank account number, but the UPIC protects sensitive banking information (i.e., the bank account number and the bank's routing/transit number), which are masked by the UPIC. Only credits to an account can be initiated with a UPIC. All debits are blocked, increasing security and control. Thus, a crook could not issue an ACH debit, write a check, or issue a demand draft.

If you are wondering if the UPIC could be used with wire transfers, the answer, at least for the present, is no. Initially, they may only be used in place of ACH credits.

Getting Started

If your vendors need instructions on how to get started, direct them to their banks. UPICs can be obtained from a participating bank. Most major banks will be able to facilitate this transaction. Contact your customer relationship manager or branch manager to find out if the bank issues UPICs.

It does not take long for the UPIC to be activated. Generally, 24 hours after the application, the number will be live. It should be communicated with the universal routing and transit number (URT) for the bank. To be certain your vendor gets this right, the bank providing the UPIC should verify the URT.

Benefits

If your customer is still dragging its feet, you can point out some of the following advantages of ACH:

- Eliminates the risk of lost or damaged checks sent in the mail
- Increases cash flow because customers will receive funds faster, generally on settlement day
- Eliminates nonsufficient funds (NSF) checks and the worry about checks bouncing
- Reduces processing costs because ACHs cost next to nothing to receive
- Gains efficiencies because fewer hands touch the payment reducing headcount;
- Lowers banking fees because there is no need for lockbox and other check services

- Enables automatic reconciliation because receiving electronic payments is the first step toward attaining straight-through processing.

Moving Forward

Once a company has obtained a UPIC, it can take aggressive action to solicit electronic payments. Some experts recommend that companies include their UPIC, along with the UTR, on their invoices much in the same way as some forward-thinking companies include their tax identification number (TIN).

IVR/IWR

Calls from vendors wondering about the status of their invoice and ensuing payment are a huge problem for many accounts payable departments. Depending on the process, they may either lack the information to answer the query, requiring that they make several phone calls to get the answer, or if they do have the information, it may require looking through files to retrieve it.

What if your suppliers could get this information without bothering anyone in accounts payable? In many organizations, this might save one or two employees who could be assigned to more value-added work. With the use of electronic invoicing and imaging and workflow, the process just got one step easier. But before we discuss how, let's look at a little history.

For many people, ordering a prescription from the pharmacy simply involves picking up the phone and punching in a series of numbers, usually their prescription numbers, phone numbers, and the time they wish to pick up their prescriptions. This technology was applied to payment information some years ago. It is called interactive voice recognition (IVR) and was used at some companies, starting 10 to 15 years ago, to give their customers and purchasing executives information about expected payments. The information was available 24/7 to anyone who had a phone and needed passwords and user IDs. It was a bit pricey, but those who used it loved it. It also helped vendors with their cash planning.

As the Internet became a more common business tool, this vendor inquiry application found its way into many of the electronic invoicing modules. Accounts payable departments love it because not only does it eliminate many (but not all) of the calls coming into the department from vendors looking for money, but it also tells the vendors where the invoice and check are in the process. Thus, if the invoice has been sent (electronically) to purchasing for approval and that approval has not been received, the vendors will see that and can call purchasing. As you might imagine, accounts payable likes the fact that purchasing can no longer claim to have sent something in that was never sent. Of course, the shoe is sometimes on the other foot when purchasing did approve the invoice two weeks earlier and someone in accounts payable messes up.

CONCLUSION

Technology has made huge inroads in the payment arena, helping the accounts payable department become more efficient. The applications discussed in this chapter have come down tremendously in price, putting them within reach of most organizations, and they come in many variations. For example, an organization that is not capable of or willing to do its own imaging might choose to outsource that function on a per-item basis. As of spring 2006, at least one organization will accept all of your invoices at a lockbox set up for your vendors, image them for you, and send them to you via e-mail in less than 24 hours. The cost of this robust application is a mere 30 cents per item. Technology has become relatively inexpensive and is raising the productivity of the fine staffs that work in accounts payable.

16

Cash Management Initiatives

Accounts payable definitely has a cash flow/cash management component. Controllers and CFOs are well aware of the financial implications of the timing of the outflow of cash. In addition to the obvious cash planning strategies, there are several tactics your staff could use to improve your organization's cash position, as well as one or two that will inadvertently harm your cash flow situation (see the Clean Desk Syndrome section).

CASH MANAGEMENT INITIATIVES

Your accounts payable department can take on the following projects to improve the cash flow of your organization:

- *Move payments from a check process to an ACH payment mechanism.* Work with suppliers to renegotiate payment terms, adding a few days to the standard terms. Not only will you greatly reduce your check production costs, but you will also improve supplier relations and increase your cash position slightly.

215

- *Thoroughly research any items you think are escheatable to uncover any that are legitimately yours and do not have to be turned over to the state.* Make sure you document everything. You can get an early start on this project by routinely researching all checks that remain uncashed for 90 days. This will not only improve your cash flow, but it will also help when it comes time to do your state reporting for unclaimed property.

- *Claim any unclaimed property that belongs to your organization and has been turned over to the state.* How can you do that? Get online and go to *www.missingmoney.com* or *www.naupa .org/mainframe.asp?VisitorType=owner*, as not every state participates in the missingmoney.com Web site.

- *Take every early-payment discount offered by your suppliers.* Track those that you miss and research why the discount was missed. Once you' have identified the cause, take the necessary action to make sure that problem does not repeat itself, causing your organization to lose the discount. Unless interest rates rise significantly, this is a no-lose proposition for all companies, even those in a borrowing position. Taking the discount on 2/10 net 30 terms translates into a 36% rate of return, something few organizations are earning today.

- *Do everything possible to minimize the number of priority (Rush/ ASAP) checks.* Not only are Rush checks expensive to produce, but they also lead to a horrendous number of duplicate payments, which is definitely not good for cash flow.

- *Don't forget to periodically request statements from vendors, insisting that the statements show all activity, including open credits.* Once you have identified open credits, either request a check for those items or use them against open invoices. Again, document everything or the vendor may claim a short payment at some time in the future, and without your documentation, you could lose that credit.

216

CLEAN DESK SYNDROME

Some people don't like to go home at night with any work remaining unfinished. This is an admirable trait in most instances, but it can lead to trouble in some accounts payable systems. If your system allows your staff to enter an invoice for payment and then schedule it, this should not be a problem for your staff, assuming they are using the scheduling module correctly. However, in some organizations, especially those with home-grown, multipatched systems, invoices are processed for payment as soon as they are entered into the system. In these cases, when your industrious processors enter all invoices as soon as they receive them, thinking they are doing a good thing, they are actually costing you thousands, if not millions, of dollars per year. In these organizations, a clean desk in accounts payable is not necessarily a desirable thing.

SCHEDULING PAYMENTS

Payments should be scheduled according to the payment terms negotiated with the supplier. Checks should be cut early enough in the cycle to allow sufficient time to get the checks signed and mailed, if hand signatures are required. Unfortunately, when hand signatures are needed, the process necessitates collating the printed check with the backup that was provided by the original requestor. The purpose of this is to provide the check signer with the necessary information to verify that the check is accurate and to sign the check. No check signer should sign a check without this backup.

As alluded to previously, this manual process can take a considerable amount of time, depending on the number of checks and the rest of the work for the department. Additionally, hunting down authorized signers, getting them to review and sign the checks, separating those checks from the backup, and putting them in envelopes for mailing can take time.

Thus, it is sometimes necessary to schedule checks for printing a week or two before the due date. This will provide adequate time for the staff to get the work done and still get the checks to the suppliers in a timely manner, allowing your organization to maintain good relations with your vendors and not get put on credit hold.

PAYMENT TIMING: IS IT STRETCHING OR TIMING?

Stretching payments, also referred to by some as payment timing, is an issue that has both hard-core proponents as well as those who vehemently object to the practice. Of course, there is a difference between the company that stretches payments because it is undergoing a hopefully temporary cash crunch and one that is stretching payments simply to fatten its already overflowing coffers.

To help judge marketplace sentiment and practice, accounts payable professionals were asked for their comments both on what their organizations are doing and what they think companies should do in this regard. A number of the respondents also piped up with additional commentary on these and related practices.

Market Practice

While some see payment stretching almost as breaking a promise to their suppliers, others see it as a standard business practice. The majority report they do not stretch payments unless forced to do so by cash flow considerations. Here's what the respondents said:

- We never stretch payments. 42.5%
- We stretch payments when we run into periods of tight cash flow but immediately revert to paying at or near terms when cash is not in short supply. 20%

218

- We have a formal (monitored) payment stretching policy as part of our cash management policy. 15%
- We have an informal payment stretching policy. 15%
- We stretch payments only when we want to window dress the financial statements. 7.5%
- We stretch payments in times of tight cash and to window dress financial statements. 0%

Market Sentiment

Contrast the practices with the respondents' personal beliefs regarding these practices. They were given all of the following statements and asked to select all that they agreed with:

- It is okay to stretch payments as a cash management initiative if you inform your suppliers. 24.24%
- It is okay to stretch payments when cash is in short supply. 21.21%
- Stretching payments is morally wrong. 18.18%
- Payment stretching is a legitimate cash management initiative. 13.64%
- Stretching payments is a necessity in a competitive environment because everyone else is doing it. 10.61%
- It is okay to stretch payments if you want to hold on to cash longer, even if there are no cash flow issues. 7.58%
- It is okay to stretch payments as a cash management initiative without informing suppliers. 4.55%

Interestingly enough, although almost two-thirds either never stretch or only do so if they are forced by cash flow considerations, only 18% think the practice is morally wrong. However, only 4.55% believe it is okay to stretch as a cash management initiative without informing suppliers.

Some organizations take the following stance described by one respondent: "If a vendor doesn't call you looking for payment, then they are okay with your timing." However, this person understands the internal consternation that can arise as a result. So once vendors begin calling looking for their money, they are put back to terms to reduce the phone interruptions to accounts payable.

It's not only the customers who can be aggressive when it comes to payments. "How about the converse," wrote one indignant respondent, "slapping 18% or higher annual 'late fees' on every invoice even if it is just one day past due from date of invoice, not even date of delivery of goods. It may even be the vendor's fault because of pricing issues, but they still slap the late fee on because: (1) it's a supplier of limited availability goods and (2) most customers won't bother to fight the nickel and dime charges as it takes more time and money than the charges themselves."

Cash Flow Considerations

When cash is tight, companies are faced with an interesting dilemma. Is this something you want to admit to your suppliers? "We are having a big cash flow issue right now," explained one respondent. This individual indicated that most vendors were okay with the stretching as long as they could talk to someone in accounts payable and find out that their invoice had been approved and was in the system, even if it couldn't be paid right away. This is an important consideration and could help in another situation. Vendors who know their invoice is in the system are less likely to send along another invoice, which savvy readers know can lead to duplicate payments.

This view was echoed by another respondent who wrote that "Stretching payments due to a temporary cash shortage would be okay only if the suppliers are informed and accept the arrangement. Most will if the situation is explained and you are upfront about the reasons." However, this person was emphatic that merely stretching payments without cash issues and without informing the suppliers was morally wrong.

Legal Considerations

Another respondent from Texas pointed out that for some governmental entities, payment stretching isn't an option, it's a legally mandated requirement. The particulars provided by that person are:

- The State of Texas requires that all payments issued against state monies be issued on the 30th day following the latter of the date the invoice was received in acceptable condition, or the date the goods/services were delivered and accepted. That's a simplified version of the law, it's actually a bit more involved than that.

- There are very few exceptions to that rule, and they are explicitly spelled-out by the agency responsible for governing state disbursements.

- An explanation of the Texas law is included in the New Vendor Packet, sent out any time the organization begins working with a new vendor. How much of this packet is read by the vendor is not clear, but in this case it is assumed they do since they return the other paperwork in the packet (e.g., W-9, EFT form, Vendor data sheet) and file our Sales Tax Certificate.

- The Texas law provides for automatic late-payment interest payments. This provision means that in the last seven years, I've had maybe one vendor argue with me about it.

The practices explained by this respondent should be emulated by any organization regardless of terms. By explaining to the vendors exactly what they can expect from your organization, you are laying the groundwork for a strong relationship.

The Dissidents

As you might imagine, there were some rather vehement comments about the payment stretching issue. A few representative viewpoints are:

- If there is an issue with a particular invoice and the vendor has been notified, it is okay to stretch the payment until the issue is resolved. If, however, the invoice is legitimate as well as accurate, it is wrong to stretch the payment.
- I can understand stretching payments, even though I don't agree with the practice. Vendors need their money to pay their vendors and on down the line. If you agree with the 30-day terms, then that's when you should pay.
- I prefer to pay my suppliers within terms, but I am instructed by management that I must cut back on how much I pay out daily, because it is getting close to the end of the quarter, and so on.

CONCLUSION

Without a doubt, this is a topic where no consensus exists within the industry. Interestingly, payment timing does not appear to be an industry practice, and even those who use it believe informing the supplier is a crucial element of a successful program.

17

Sarbanes-Oxley and Certifications

The Sarbanes-Oxley Act of 2002 is comprised of 66 sections, only a few of which directly affect the way the accounts payable function is handled. The intent was not only to close the loopholes that made fraudulent transgressions possible, but also to hold management at the very highest levels responsible for what went on in their companies on their watch.

It was inevitable that increased accountability, in the form of fines and possible jail time, would trickle down to middle management. Few officers would willingly sign financial statements under such dire threats without requiring some sort of a guarantee from the minions who toiled on their behalf. Thus, quickly, subcertifications sprung up. These documents, also known as cascading certifications or upstream certifications (depending on where you stand), are now found at a significant percentage of the companies we interviewed.

OVERVIEW OF THE ACT

The Act is broken into 11 main parts called Titles. Each of the Titles is further subdivided into portions called Sections. The most famous of the sections are probably:

- Whistleblower Protections a.k.a. Retaliation against informants
- Auditor Independence
- Timely Disclosures
- Corporate Responsibility for financial reports
- Management Assessment of internal controls

While the whistleblower piece may be the second most interesting section, it does not greatly affect the accounts payable operations. Similarly, while it might be great fun to talk about CEOs and CFOs getting fined and possibly going to jail, we are not going to spend a whole lot of time discussing either of these issues. The main focus of this chapter will be on internal controls Section 404 and, to a somewhat lesser extent, Section 302 (Corporate Responsibility for financial reports).

MANAGEMENT ASSESSMENT OF INTERNAL CONTROLS

This innocuous-sounding section has sparked a revolution in many accounts payable departments around the country. The requirement is simply that annual financial reports must include an "Internal Control Report," which states that management is responsible for adequate internal control structure and an assessment by management of the effectiveness of the control structure. Shortcomings in the controls must also be reported.

Now, with the sword of Damocles hanging over management's head in the form of fines and jail time, it is not likely that they will simply sign off without a thorough and exhaustive review. In many cases, they are not signing off until they have their managers sign off on similar documents. It is not likely that these subcertifications will bind their signers in the same way that the CEO and CFO are bound if they certify fraudulent statements, but the end result will not be good if there are errors or worse. Not only do the top executives have to sign off, but the external auditors must also attest to the accuracy of the company management's claim that the internal accounting controls are:

- In place
- Operational
- Effective

Specifically, the Act requires that the annual report contain an internal control report that:

- States the responsibility of management for establishing and maintaining an adequate internal control structure and procedures for financial reporting
- Contains an assessment, as of the end of the most recent fiscal year of the issuer, of the effectiveness of the internal control structure and procedures of the issuer for financial reporting

It is important to note that these assessments are part of the annual report. These requirements, along with the harsh penalties for fraud or misrepresentation, have lead some companies to require subcertifications from their managers who are responsible for internal controls at the operational levels.

AUDITORS' ASSESSMENT OF INTERNAL CONTROLS

In the past, especially in a captive situation, the auditors might have been persuaded to sign off when in their hearts they believed something was amiss. Those days have ended. With the demise of one accounting firm and most of the other big ones facing lawsuits from disgruntled investors who relied on their work in the past, auditors are no longer caving to the demands of their corporate clients.

It should also be noted that the public accounting firm hired to audit the books and prepare the annual report must also make the internal control assessment. The audit and the internal control assessment go hand in hand. They may not be separate. There is no passing the buck or fingerpointing allowed here. Specifically, the Act requires that the firm that prepares or issues the audit report shall attest to and report on the assessment made by the management of the firm it has audited. The net result is that stringent internal controls are finally finding their way into the corners of most accounts payable departments.

AUDIT TRAILS

Audit trails are important across all functions in accounts payable. Being able to document decisions regarding sales and use tax, unclaimed property, and W-9 and 1042s are just the beginning of why documentation is important. While your accountants may want the audit trail information, government auditors will insist on it if you come up for an audit by one of these groups or if you are charged a penalty for failure to comply with certain regulations. The audit trail will be important in avoiding fines as it will demonstrate your intent.

RECORDS RETENTION

Records retention policies go hand in hand with audit trails. You can't have a decent audit trail if records cannot be retrieved. In many organizations, this is a much bigger problem than most would expect. Even the very largest companies—the ones that you would expect would be able to put their hand on any record they could conceivably need at a moment's notice—

run into trouble on this one. While electronic initiatives will take care of some of the control points surrounding records retention, this will only happen if the appropriate control points are properly addressed. This translates into proper indexing and storage routines.

When *Accounts Payable Now & Tomorrow* polled a group of its readers about their records retention policies, more than one-quarter of them indicated that they had improved those policies in light of Sarbanes-Oxley.

Your record retention policies should conform to IRS and other governmental agency requirements. Here are some documents you might want to refer to in this regard:

- For overall retention of books and records information, IRS Revenue Procedure 97-22
- For information about electronic information, IRS Revenue Procedure 98-25

Being able to access these records will become very important if you end up with sales and use tax or unclaimed property auditors in your office.

When a new accounting system is installed or, for that matter, when the existing one is upgraded, care needs to be taken to ensure that no information is lost. As a word of caution, most duplicate payment experts see a bonanza for themselves whenever a new accounting system is installed, because there is typically a breakdown in controls and more items than normal get paid twice. Recognizing that this may occur is the first preventative step companies can take. Identifying those potential duplicates before they go out the door is the next step.

POLICY AND PROCEDURES MANUAL

Like the semiannual visit to the dentist, most professionals know they should have one but only a small percentage actually do. Even in those organizations that finally do get one put together, it is rarely updated. While Sarbanes-Oxley doesn't actually mandate a policy and procedures manual for accounts payable, it's hard to visualize many situations where one would be considered in compliance without one.

Prepare a flowchart documenting all processes within the department. With this document, a good portion of the work producing the manual has been completed. The task at hand is converting that diagram into words, keeping it updated, and making sure it reflects what actually goes on in the department.

What sometimes happens, with both the manual and the flowchart, is that over time, processes drift from the documented policy to something else. Unfortunately, that something else often introduces weaknesses and control points into the process. Sometimes, in an effort to speed the work up, steps are omitted from the process or the segregation of duties requirements are voided.

The policy and procedures manual should be shared with all affected parties. This means that, for example, purchasing should have input into and be given the final version of all sections that affect it. It is meaningless to write a policy that will require a three-day turnaround time of invoices, if interoffice mail is used and it is slow. Similarly, if the purchasing manager is required to approve all invoices and he travels extensively, a lengthy approval time will be required unless electronic mechanisms are used or the Board authorization for spending approvals can be further delegated.

Many organizations now post their accounts payable policy and procedures manual on their company intranet sites. This makes the information available to anyone who needs it, makes updating it relatively easy, and keeps it on the forefront of everyone's minds. It also makes it easy to refer people with questions to the manual rather than have accounts payable answer every question. From a control standpoint, this is recommended. It forces everyone to the same source document for procedures, rather than relying on one individual's memory, which may or may not be accurate.

Note that having a policy and procedures manual can come back to haunt you if the staff does not adhere to it. By posting it on the company intranet, or making it readily available using some other mechanism, the department is announcing its requirements. It makes it relatively easy to uncover situations where the policy is not adhered to by the accounts payable staff.

SEGREGATION OF DUTIES

In order to perpetrate a fraud through accounts payable, it is frequently necessary to have access to more than one function. For example, a person would have to have access to the check stock and the facsimile signer. Thus one of the easiest ways to prevent fraud is to assign responsibilities in such a manner to minimize this risk. Depending on the size of the department, it may be necessary to work with another group to achieve this goal.

Alternatively, close scrutiny on a regular basis of any person with multiple conflicting responsibilities is recommended. Companies sometimes get lulled into a false sense of security because the particular employee with multiple conflicting responsibilities has been with the company for a long time. This is a mistake because most frauds are committed by longtime trusted employees.

ELIMINATE REALLY BAD ACCOUNTS PAYABLE PRACTICES

More organizations than you would suspect employ what are generally considered really bad practices in some parts of their process. Many of these are inherited practices ("we always did it that way"), and others are a result of corporate culture ("boys will be boys"). Whatever the reason, Sarbanes-Oxley has shone its light on these dirty little secrets, and at least some of the organizations that tolerated these practices are finally letting go of them. Before listing them, we have to salute the accounts payable professionals who seized the opportunity presented by Sarbanes-Oxley and used the Act as ammunition to get rid of the practices. Here are just a few of them:

- A petty cash box
- Dubious T&E reimbursement practices
- Not enforcing the T&E policy equitably across the board
- Not using positive pay
- Not using a duplicate payment audit firm because the company "never makes duplicate payments" (since these firms almost always work on a contingency basis, why not verify that claim?)
- Allowing frequent Rush checks to cover employee sloppiness
- Not mandating the use of a corporate T&E card
- Not requiring a W-9 before a payment is made to a vendor
- Ignoring the unclaimed property laws
- Not filing 1042 and 1042-S for payments made to nonresident aliens

You can probably identify more bad practices in your own organization. Very few groups are immune from employing one or two bad practices somewhere across their financial spectrum. Once you have identified them, try to root them out. If you need help, both your internal and external auditors are likely to be in your corner, so get their support.

MONITORING REPORTS

Establishing effective controls, unfortunately, is not a one-shot project; it is an ongoing process. To ensure that the controls remain effective and function appropriately, they need to be reviewed periodically. Additionally, and equally important, reports need to be designed to ensure that the controls function as they should. They are also part of the control process. These reports can be best designed by figuring out where the potential weaknesses are in the process.

For example, one of the most common ways for an employee to commit check fraud is for the employee to simply change the mailing address of a vendor in the master vendor file. Then, once the check has been mailed, the employee with access to the master vendor file goes back into the system and changes the address back to the correct address. It often takes months for it to come to light that the check went to the wrong vendor and an even longer time to track down where the check did go. If the employee is smart, he or she will have covered the tracks by that time.

How can you uncover this little scheme? A report of all changes to the master vendor file should be run each week (or month), and the report should be reviewed by someone at a fairly senior level not related to the process. By looking at all the changes, this little scheme would be uncovered. The problem with this approach is that few executives at senior levels want to wade through the minutia of the changes made to the master vendor file.

Review your own processes and find the applicable weak spots and then design your own reports. Depending on your processes, you may need a few or many such reports. For example, if inactive vendors are infrequently (or heaven forbid, never) deactivated in the master vendor file, you will need to review any activity in formerly inactive accounts. A shrewd employee might use one of these accounts, along with some address changes to the master vendor file, to submit a phony invoice, get it approved, and then maneuver your organization's money into his or her bank account.

REAL-WORLD OBSERVATIONS

Anecdotal evidence suggests that auditors reviewing accounts payable operations are having problems with two key areas. They would like to see a greater segregation of duties, which is sometimes difficult if the organization has only a handful of employees working in the department. This becomes difficult when you factor in vacations and backup requirements.

The other area that sometimes does not come out smelling like a rose is the area of documentation. Often a department will have a policy manual but will not update it as changes are made to the daily policies and procedures. Worse, employees occasionally will develop their own workarounds. This leaves the department open to criticism if these workarounds actually weaken the internal controls as they make the employee's processes run a little smoother. Finally, there can be a problem when different employees in the same department handle the same task in different manners.

Thus, it is a good idea to review how employees are performing each task and then compare that to the written policies and procedures manual. They should match, and if they don't, the necessary corrections should be made.

About *Accounts Payable Now & Tomorrow*

Accounts Payable Now & Tomorrow is a monthly publication devoted to payment issues. Each issue will contain:

- Four to six hard-hitting articles offering practical advice to the many problematic issues confronting payables operations everywhere
- Two Guest Columns from the most-respected names in their fields covering specialty functions including: 1099s, sales and use tax, unclaimed property, p-cards, VAT, banking issues (positive pay, ACH, Check 21, etc.), accounting issues (yes, Sarbanes-Oxley, internal controls etc.), fraud, software and audits, and more
- A Tips, Tactics, and Strategies section . . . and much more

With your paid subscription, you'll also get a weekly e-zine, *e-News from the AP Front*, a quick-read e-mail update, the opportunity to participate in and get the results from ground-breaking research focused on payment issues.

To receive a sample copy of the print publication, send an e-mail to publisher@ap-now.com with the words "Wiley sent me" in the subject line. Make sure you include your company name, title, and mailing address.

If you would prefer to just be added to the distribution of the complimentary e-zine, simply send the same information with a note to that effect to publisher@ap-now.com

Index

Index

Index

Index